THE
SUMO
ADVANTAGE

LEVERAGING BUSINESS DEVELOPMENT

TO TEAM WITH HEAVYWEIGHTS

AND GROW IN ANY ECONOMY

THE
SUMO
ADVANTAGE

BERNIE BRENNER
COFOUNDER OF TRUECAR.COM

FOREWORD BY CHIP PERRY
FORMER CEO, AUTOTRADER.COM

MOMENTUM@WORK PRESS
AUSTIN, TX

© 2014 Bernie Brenner

Published by
Momentum@Work Press
Austin, TX

Publisher's Cataloging-in-Publication Data
Brenner, Bernie.

   The Sumo advantage : leveraging business development to team with heavyweights and grow in any economy / Bernie Brenner. – Austin, TX : Momentum@Work Press, 2014.

   p. ; cm.

   ISBN13: 978-0-9860460-0-1

   1. Strategic alliances (Business) 2. Business networks--Management. 3. New business enterprises--Management. 4. Small business--Management. 5. Success in business. I. Title.

   HD69.S8 B74 2014
   650.13-dc23   2013945010

FIRST EDITION

Project coordination by Jenkins Group, Inc.
www.BookPublishing.com

Interior design by Brooke Camfield

Printed in the United States of America
18   17   16   15   14 • 5 4 3 2 1

CONTENTS

Foreword   vii

Preface   xi

Acknowledgments   xv

Introduction   xvii

Part I: Business Development as a Business Generator

1   The Four Distinctions   3

2   The BD Layer—Your Company's Turbocharger   19

Part II: How You Get a Deal

3   Finding Your Sumo   31

4   Gaining and Maintaining Control—A MUST   43

5   Courting the Sumo   55

6   Creating Confusion   67

7   Tying the Knot with Your Sumo   79

Part III: Keeping an Eye on the Long-Term Potential

8	Managing Strategic Partners	97
9	The Best Partner Development Managers (PDMs)	113
10	The BD-Centric Organization	129
11	Strategic Thinking—Leverage Your Killer App	137
12	From Planning to Execution	145
	About the Author	151

FOREWORD

BY CHIP PERRY,

Former CEO, AutoTrader.com

T oday's complex business environment is challenging all companies, big and small, to find creative new ways to grow and evolve their business. One effective strategy that savvy companies are using is partnering with other companies. However, as we all know, successful partnering is easier said than done. Most companies are sales-driven and empower either their product or sales executives to drive the corporate strategy and growth process. Frequently these efforts fail because they are missing a key ingredient . . . a "business development" mind-set and culture. What is a business development mind-set and culture? you might ask.

It is a topic of great interest to me since it helped AutoTrader.com grow from zero to more than $1 billion in revenues between 1997 and 2013, and from a fledgling start-up company to the market leader in the online auto shopping and advertising industry. As the company's first employee as well as AutoTrader.com's president and CEO during that time, I was deeply involved in the many partnerships we pursued. As a brand new business with very few linkages to AutoTrader's print operations, we had to assemble an entire ecosystem of automotive content, data analysis, consumer shopping tools, dealer software, and marketing partnerships to get the company off the ground. Business development was essential to AutoTrader.com's growth and success and should be a core strategy for any entrepreneurial venture. Fortunately, Bernie Brenner has written the quintessential guide to business development. *The Sumo Advantage* which is a unique addition to any growth-oriented CEO's, CMO's or strategy officer's bookshelf. Many of the recent books about "business development," or "deal making," or "partnership strategy and negotiations," are written from a tactical perspective or are academic treatises about strategic planning. They are not guides to developing and executing an effective business development strategy. *The Sumo Advantage*, on the other hand, is.

The Sumo Advantage describes in very clear and concrete terms how a company should think about, identify, negotiate and manage strategic partnerships as a tool for finding new avenues for growth and competitive advantage. In addition, the book is rooted in the belief that for a partnership to be successful and sustainable over the long term it must be a win-win for both parties.

Although written for entrepreneurs who are seeking to build partnerships with larger companies—the Sumos in their industry or an adjacent one—this book will benefit executives from *both* small and large companies. As it richly illustrates, small companies can benefit mightily from leveraging the resources, capabilities, and credibility of larger Sumo-sized organizations. At the same time, *The Sumo Advantage* can be an essential resource for large companies as well who recognize the need to look outside their four walls to find partnerships with smaller, more nimble companies who are approaching customers from a different perspective or are meeting their needs with innovative new technologies. The tools and tactics and thought processes espoused in this book will be useful to executives in companies of all sizes.

The Sumo Advantage effectively makes the case that business development is different from the sales function. In fact, the mind-set and techniques that salespeople use to grow revenue are frequently poorly suited to the demands of the business development function. Applying tried-and-true sales techniques to business development won't work, nor will using business development tactics in a sales environment. They are two completely different but complementary business functions.

The book thoroughly dissects all aspects of business development and explains how you can leverage it to your advantage. Readers learn how it can be a major driver of business strategy, how it can affect changes in industry structure, how a potential partner who might be reluctant to engage in deal talks can be brought to the table, how to reel in the partner via selective disclosure of information that piques the partner's interest, how to employ ambiguity in deal negotiations to achieve a good result, and how to effectively manage a partnership with skilled Partner Development Managers (PDMs) after the deal is done. I am sure you will find the content in this book to be new and refreshing as you ponder you next big partnership deal.

I witnessed Bernie's remarkable deal-making skills up close and personal. He was always a gentleman while also being a highly persistent, forceful, and creative partner and negotiator. In this book, among many valuable points, Bernie talks about the importance of not getting to a "no" in a negotiation, which is a critical nuance in the deal-making process. As I look back on the deals we did together, although he cleverly didn't reveal his Sumo Advantage framework to me at the time, I can definitely see the earmarks of his techniques in the partnerships we created. Although we often started at "no," by the time Bernie was done, we were definitely saying "yes!" You will be too.

—Chip Perry

PREFACE

su·mo

[soo-moh] noun

A Japanese form of wrestling in which a contestant loses if he is forced out of the ring, or if any part of his body except the soles of his feet touches the ground; contestants usually being men of great height and weight [Source: Dictionary.com].

ad·van·tage

[ad-van-tij] noun

1. Any means especially favorable to success.
2. Benefit; gain; profit.
3. Superiority or ascendancy.

The Sumo Advantage
business term

1. An entrepreneur's alignment with a major market force, capability, or accelerator with the intent to grow market share and crush the competition.

2. A business effort that is extremely difficult to achieve but when done correctly propels an entrepreneur to a growth phase virtually impossible to replicate.

Entrepreneurs and business owners alike constantly seek advantage over their competition. For most, "winning" means gaining market dominance, product superiority, or increased sales. The stated goal is often to land the "800-pound gorilla," the implication being that such a coup would alter the company's future. But is a gorilla the right target?

In fact, the largest gorilla ever recorded was not 800 pounds but 590 pounds. By comparison, the heaviest sumo wrestler ever recorded was Konishiki Yasokichi, now retired, who weighed 630 pounds. Yes, the sumo carried more weight than the largest gorilla, in more ways than one.

Unlike the gorilla, the sumo is always focused on beating the competition. He leverages his enormous weight, height, and muscle to force his competitor out of the ring—or, in business terms, out of his space. The gorilla is raw muscle and can exert enormous strength, but the gorilla is not strategic. It is instinctive and lacks self-awareness, imagination, and independent will. Partnering with a gorilla of any size is unlikely to help you achieve any real progress. The sumo, on the other hand, is interested in outpositioning, outsmarting, and even outpsyching the competition, using all means available, within the rules of engagement.

The Sumo Advantage is just that—alignment with a major market force, capability, or accelerator with the intent to generate revenue and grow market share. It's a partnership that drives momentum and revenue growth and is, most importantly, a clear and present danger to your competition. Leveraging the Sumo Advantage means your competition will need to react to you, the small, often-underfunded entrepreneur. However, whatever you lack in funding, you make up for in passion, faster response times, a big idea, and a broader vision. And now with your sumo by your side, you have the equivalent of a big brother to help you fight your fights.

Entrepreneurs by themselves rarely have the weight to deliver a knockout punch. Being thrown from the ring by a bigger opponent is a real possibility. But that all changes when you have a sumo standing beside you, who is ready to support you and help you win.

There's just one problem with this plan. Sumos are solo warriors. They enter the ring alone, ready to fight a single opponent. For that reason, striking a deal with a sumo is incredibly difficult.

Harnessing the sumo's power is not easy. Initially, he won't want you, the smaller business, sitting on his shoulders, calling the shots as if you now have everything you need to compete head-on with YOUR largest competitor. He knows his strength and the power he brings to the relationship; your goal is to demonstrate the important role you can play to his customers, despite your diminutive size. Of course, your goal is not to compete against the sumo's competitors. No, your goal is to partner with the sumo and, together, best *your own* competitors. But it has to work to the sumo's advantage, too. The sumo has to see gains in market share, competitive advantage, and product enhancements—and, sometimes, it's just about revenue. When it works, it is a thing of beauty.

Pursuing the Sumo Advantage delivers:

1. Strategic advantages
2. New paths to entry
3. Barriers for your competition
4. A valuation increase—it should at least double
5. An easier path to raising capital
6. Exponential increases to your revenue
7. Market momentum
8. The ability to crush your competition

In this book, you will learn everything you need to know about pursuing, negotiating, and signing the biggest partnership deals imaginable with sumo companies. You'll also learn the most critical component to ensuring that this successful relationship endures— how to nurture the partnership postdeal. But once you have a sumo in your corner, backing you up, the opportunities to partner with market leaders will seem unending.

ACKNOWLEDGMENTS

There are many to thank, and I am going to start with my wife, Allison. You are a person who acts with complete intention, refuses to accept "good enough" from your relationships, and raises everyone's level of consciousness. To my son Mac, you are the sweetest boy on this planet. To my daughter Charlotte, your soul is filled with so much wisdom. And to my daughter Sabrina, you teach us all with how you gain so much happiness in helping others.

Thanks to Michael Meyer, John Carney, Simon Rakoff and John Price, four great entrepreneurs who have inspired me to do more, including writing this book.

To my TrueCar (formerly Zag.com) founding partners, Scott Painter, Tom Taira, Jim Nguyen, and Greg Brogger, we've been through so many highs and lows with the company over the past eight years. Those stories will make a great book one day.

To my kick-ass BD team at TrueCar, we have built a BD Layer that many cannot claim to have achieved. You are this book, and I thank you for giving me the experiences to author the following ideas.

Jason Nierman, my little brother, you make me proud. Dave Pributsky, you are the essence of Spidey Sense. Allyson Geber, there is truly no better hunter than YOU. And to Steve "The Moretti," thanks for your friendship and for choosing to be part of this team. And a very special thank you to Jacqueline Livingston, my rock at the office.

To those who made a difference in my business career: Bobby Shaw, for passing on your relationship-building skills while at MCA; Dick Raines, for providing a great environment in which to thrive; and Bob Sofsky, my first angel investor who is now my great big brother.

Finally, to my mom, the hardest-working entrepreneur I know. Thanks for showing me how to work so hard and achieve my goals. I love you.

INTRODUCTION

Many businesspeople use the terms "sales" and "business development" interchangeably. They think the two phrases refer to the same process with the same potential results. Granted, the two words together—"business" and "development"—could vaguely refer to any method of creating business, but when people use them to mean "grow revenue quickly," they're really referring to sales. But sales is not *developing* the business; sales is solely about generating income. Business development (BD), on the other hand, is more strategic; it's not just about the money to be earned. So the people who use the two terms synonymously are, plain and simply, wrong.

While there is a place for both BD and sales within most companies, the skill set required, prospecting approach, deal structure, business process, and potential impact on the company are worlds apart. Use a typical sales approach to pursue a BD deal and I guarantee that, at best, you'll get a crappy outcome, relative to what you thought this so-called powerhouse deal could do for your company. Conversely, take a BD tack with a sales deal and you'll rarely ever close it efficiently, because they are completely at odds with each other. It's the wrong approach.

On the one hand, sales is all about offering tangible goods and services available for purchase—items many companies have already identified as something they need. Sales is about developing revenue for the company in the short term by finding buyers for clearly defined products and services. I always use paper cups as an example. Most companies know what paper cups are, know whether they need them, can clearly describe their features and benefits, and have a budget line item for them. So the role of sales is to persuade the customer to buy your cups instead of someone else's. Why? Because you already know that the company is going to buy cups from *somebody*. Your challenge is to convince the buyer that your products make the most sense for his or her particular need and then seal the deal with a purchase order.

BD is the polar opposite of sales. It's about selling a vision of the future—of what could be—for a potential partner willing to collaborate with you. It's about defining what we can do together that neither company is doing today to serve a third customer. You're not selling tangible products and services to another company in BD; you're proposing a partnership in pursuit of bigger opportunities elsewhere. That's the biggest difference between sales and BD, but there are several other important distinctions as well.

In BD, the business process is strategic, not transactional, and no money changes hands between partners. Your potential partner, which is typically an industry heavyweight (what I'm calling a sumo), and your ultimate customer may have given no thought whatsoever to the benefits your proposal can reap. So there are no incentives related to consummating a deal with you. It's even more likely that sumos will try to discourage future contact from you; they prefer to compete solo. Making any headway at all in forging a business relationship with your potential BD partners can take months, even years. And yet, when the relationship is formalized and collaboration begins, the rewards are often pivotal for the companies involved. Your company's valuation can double or triple with a successful BD deal. It's a growth catapult.

A single sales contract rarely has the same impact. But let's be very clear here. The purpose of BD is to help accelerate your sales—think of it as a platform or springboard. The BD Layer, which is something I'll get into more detail about in the next chapter, will accelerate your revenue through faster, greater, more profitable sales.

BD ADVANTAGES

So how, exactly, do you leverage business development to accelerate growth in your business? Keep in mind that partnering with sumos can achieve a number of different goals for your business. Your goal may be revenue generation, or market share increase, or tapping into a sumo's resources to avoid duplication of effort. Your goal may be to adopt your partner company's best practices in a particular area of their business where you feel yours is weaker, or to gain access to their technology, or to develop a lower-cost customer acquisition model, or to build increased credibility in your space, for example. The point is accelerating growth in your business can be accomplished in a number of ways beyond pure revenue generation; sales isn't the only option. It all depends on what your business goals are and how your partner can best help you achieve them.

In the end, your sales results will skyrocket when you use an effective BD strategy. Here's an example of how to create a BD Layer, which goes beyond just thinking about sales. SpareFoot.com, a company I advise on BD, is a great early stage company in Austin, Texas. It is a business-to-consumer (B2C) marketplace for more than 8,000 storage facilities across the country. Consumers in need of a storage facility can turn to SpareFoot for a profile of the location and the available units in their local area. This extends way beyond U-haul and Public Storage, the titans in the storage industry. By forging this network of independent storage facilities, SpareFoot is helping to elevate the competitiveness of the smaller players.)

But SpareFoot is doing more than helping independent storage facilities find customers. It is also helping other, much larger, companies expand their product lines into storage. One such example is truck rentals, since a high number of people moving to another home generally need to move some of their "stuff" into or out of storage facilities. So SpareFoot partnered with sumo Penske Truck Rental and now connects consumers seeking a truck rental with storage facilities, as well as helping its storage facility operators gain access to Penske trucks for their own customers.

SpareFoot had a huge opportunity to partner. It created a BD Layer to connect its service—information about storage space—with related services provided by market leaders to the same customer base. Why is it better to pursue a partnership versus a product development initiative? A partnership will reduce risk, provide expertise, minimize distractions, lower costs, and help your company to focus on its core competency and scalability. By pursuing a partnership with an established company, such as Penske, SpareFoot has filled two voids in the market and made its position much stronger.

The reason such a partnership makes sense for Penske is that it receives inbound calls for truck rental reservations every day. Now, through SpareFoot, Penske has a nationwide network of storage facilities that booking agents can bundle with the truck rental transaction. SpareFoot's sales will potentially skyrocket by putting Penske Truck Rental customers directly into the SpareFoot network.

Besides not having to invest huge sums of money in a start-up operation, such as with a truck rental business, a second advantage of partnering with a sumo is the barrier to entry you're establishing for your competitors. If you spent the time and money to set up your own product, you're telling your competition that it's not tough to do. But if you partner with a major player to leverage *their* capabilities, you're signaling to your competitors that it's hard, but you just leapfrogged them by partnering with the best. And to beat you, they're going to have to best your partner—your sumo—which is a daunting challenge. As a start-up, you suddenly have scale, experience, and additional resources to supplement your (perhaps) limited funding.

A third advantage of partnering is the validation and authority you've just earned by aligning yourself with a Fortune 500 or Fortune 100 company—your sumo. Given the herd mentality, when others see that you've partnered with a major player, they'll perceive you to be more established. They'll also assume your idea is a smart one, since your Fortune 500 partner wants to be involved. The respect your partner receives in the marketplace is now transferred to you. And passing the rigorous due diligence process corporations insist on is now an asset for your business and your investors. You've gained instant credibility through your strategic partner, which, in the end, helps the execution of your sales strategy.

I launched my charity using this BD philosophy as well. I have a very deep appreciation for those in our country who keep us safe. Military men and women, police, and firefighters, who I refer to as America's heroes, all deserve massive recognition for taking on a career that puts their lives on the line in the normal course of work. That's a job I don't have, and I would have concern (yet support) if one of my children chose such a path.

As a result of this feeling, I have been buying this group lunch whenever I can. If they are ahead of or behind me in line for lunch,

I try to grab the check. To me, this is not charity, and I would never hand one of them cash. It is a gesture of thanks.

I started ThanksABunch.org (TAB) in 2010. TAB's goal is to facilitate an action where individuals approach these heroes, shake hands, and say "Thank you! Your next lunch is on me!" In doing so, they hand a TAB lunch card worth $50, good at over 18,000 restaurants.

As you can imagine, the big challenge in launching the program was the participation by restaurants. I could try to approach the big national chains such as McDonalds and Burger King. Those certainly are two sumos on the list. But there were inherent challenges with doing so. For example, will all franchisees accept the card? Who pays for the food—corporate or the franchisee? I need to make sure I have enough volume in place to train this network. This is a lot of effort, and it's still limited by food choice.

As a result, I approached Restaurant.com. They have 18,000 restaurants across the country trained to accept a redeemable certificate of monetary value. These locations are very diverse in geography, cuisine, and expense. Approaching this sumo was easier than most. Through a series of discussions, documents, and process flow charts, Restaurant.com agreed to be the fulfillment channel for the ThanksABunch program. On top of that, this sumo agreed to help us financially through the ongoing volume of cards.

So overnight and upon launch, ThanksABunch.org launched a nationwide platform where individuals can come to the website, purchase tax-deductible $50 cards for $10 each (yes, that's right; a $10 donation turns into an American hero receiving $50 in value), and hand them to our military personnel with a handshake gesture of thanks. TAB does not have to manage a network of restaurants, issue dynamic codes that the restaurants accept, provide any technology to support such action, etc. We, as an organization, can feel very confident that the process is handled by a capable and focused enterprise.

BD is as much about earning a solid reputation in the marketplace in a split second by partnering with a more established and respected partner as it is about increasing your top line. All the positive attributes your partner has are now yours, to a great extent. And moving forward, even after your current BD effort wraps up, your company will be light-years ahead of your competition, thanks to your partner relationships. You can now use that first BD success as a stepping-stone to bigger and more lucrative projects.

ACCELERATION ENGINE

While BD is strategic and sales is more transaction oriented, your company needs both to be successful. Don't feel you need to choose between the two functions. Instead, use them in combination to achieve even faster growth.

BD is a sales accelerator, but you need a strong sales organization to support your BD efforts if you are going to reap optimal results. BD and sales have different roles, but both contribute to a successful partnership. Where BD identifies the opportunity and forges the business partnership with an outside organization, sales is critical to the overall results of the project. BD helps create transactions, but, ultimately, it's the sales team that will get the revenue in the bank account. While BD takes the lead in getting valuation-doubling deals, sales is the transaction generator you can't live without. They work together . . . but don't try to use them at the same time.

HOW TO USE THIS BOOK

I have spoken to hundreds of CEOs about BD. Although they are curious about it, there are always a few in each group who think there is no way that the Sumo Advantage can apply to them. I'm here to tell you that it does apply, no matter what industry you're in. I'm 100 percent positive that your sumo is out there, even if you can't think of one right now. I would also submit that if you assume you have nothing to gain by partnering with a sumo, this book is even more important to you and your business.

The Sumo Advantage is filled with information about how to find and partner with sumos, but it starts by distinguishing between sales and BD. If you are unaware of the distinctions, then your sales-only focus may be what is holding you back. Understanding and really believing that sales and BD are different functions is an important first step in taking your business to the next level.

As you read and process this information, you will see that it is an interconnected system that takes patience and finesse but reaps huge rewards for companies that pursue partnerships. Resist disbelief in any one concept until you finish the book. I promise you that your perspective on the value of sumo relations, how to go after them and how to develop them will change. I'll share a story with you from one of my recent speaking engagements to drive this point home.

A CEO with a very impressive company attended one of my presentations and was not shy about sharing that he did not believe in partnerships; he made the point several times. He saw no value in them and actively enforced that belief throughout his organization. But I was determined to change his mind. So I would periodically look at him as I made various points during the presentation and could see that he not only was engaged but also wanted to hear more.

The next day he e-mailed me the following note:

Bernie,

I normally dislike our [CEO group's] speakers, but I got a lot out of your presentation. In the past, I have been telling people: "Partnerships are worth nothing; paying customers are worth everything." I think I'm ready to change my tune.

I wasn't surprised. I've heard that partnerships are worthless countless times from skeptical audience members. I've also heard:

- "I don't have millions of dollars to invest in this."
- "I'm not big enough."
- "I don't have enough resources."
- "I already do business development, and my company still is not growing."
- "How can this possibly apply to my type of business [usually law, accounting, or some other professional service]?"

This list could go on and on. Yet I know they work. I've used these same principles in companies at a number of different life stages:

- As a start-up entrepreneur with no money. I was sitting in the basement of my rental with no salary and struck two deals with multibillion-dollar companies. I raised money after that.
- With a company that was around for more than 10 years.
- As a start-up whose initiative required the need to raise millions in initial funding before anything could happen.

Read on and you can learn how to apply these principles, too.

HOW THE BOOK IS ORGANIZED

So how should you make the most of what's here? Read everything through once and then circle back to reread it or reread sections where you want more direction. I've divided the book into three main parts, starting with business generation, followed by getting a deal, and then looking ahead to long-term opportunities.

In the first part of the book, you'll learn how and why sales and BD are two totally different animals. I offer my four distinctions between sales and BD as a guide to knowing which is which, as well as recommendations for when to use each one. Then I talk about the BD Layer and how it functions to turbocharge your company's revenues.

Once you clearly understand what BD is, how it works, and what it can do for your company, I will help you start to look for sumos to partner with. Believe it or not, there are sumos all around you; you just need to start thinking a little more creatively to identify them. I offer a couple of exercises to help you do just that. After you've identified potential sumos you want to work with, I provide the guidance, and even some dialogue, to start pursuing deals with them. I explain how important maintaining control is, as well as how to use confusion to stay in control. I also talk about how to use triangular attraction, which is my term for playing one sumo off another—borrowing one's credibility and reputation to get another interested in working with you. Finally, I help you start to negotiate a deal.

While that section is the meat of the book, the last part is just as important. One sumo deal isn't enough—you need to create a steady stream of partnerships to have a significant impact on your business and your market. By managing the sumos you're working with, as well as the people on your own team, you can build profitable and lasting relationships. You may also discover a killer app within your own company—a capability that has the potential to shift the market dynamic in your favor.

As you finish the book, I'll offer some specific steps you can take now to start building a BD-centric organization, hiring the right people to make that possible, and finding sumos that will give you a huge advantage.

MY MISSION

I start every one of my speaking engagements with the following statement: "I am not a consultant! I am one of the founders and head of business development for TrueCar.com, and I LOVE what I do. I'm here because I want to teach other entrepreneurs how to leverage big strategic deals. Everything I talk about I have personally done and done successfully. This is not theory, nor is it derived from just researching other people's successes. *The Sumo Advantage* is the result of my 20-plus years of business development success doing incredibly meaningful deals for my company's growth."

I want this for you, too. What I'm going to cover in this book is BD, not merely the process of developing business but a strategic, company-altering, life-changing system, and how you can use it to transform your entrepreneurial venture into an industry powerhouse.

Are you ready?

PART I

BUSINESS DEVELOPMENT AS A BUSINESS GENERATOR

THE FOUR
DISTINCTIONS

Sustainability.

Business acceleration. It's a buzzword and a goal for many companies, especially after several years of single-digit economic growth. Fast-paced, aggressive, exponential growth—everyone wants it, but opinions are mixed about the best way to achieve it.

Can you accelerate the growth of your business by increasing sales? Maybe. Is that the best way to accelerate growth? No. Why? Because sales efforts are not strategic; they are transactional. That is, you can increase sales only three ways: (1) by finding more customers to sell to, (2) by selling larger quantities of your products and services to your existing customer base, or (3) by selling a wider variety of your company's products and services to your existing customers. It's purely a numbers game, which means it is difficult to sustain.

In the book *Good to Great*, Jim Collins talks about getting the flywheel to spin. Once it starts, it is hard to stop. That's business development. In 2012, TrueCar Inc., a company that offers a better car-buying solution for both consumers and dealers, went through

3

what most thought was a deathblow to the business. The automotive industry—dealers, dealer lobbyists, a few manufacturers, and some state regulators—tried to shut TrueCar down. The sales team's results collapsed during this time, with the dealer count dropping from a high of 5,600 to a low of 3,100. And if the 80/20 rule exists, it certainly applies here, as the largest dealer groups in the country were the ones to drop us. If revenue comes from dealers, a 45 percent drop in the number of dealers in our network should equate to a substantial drop in revenue, right? Not in our case. Not with the BD Layer in place.

While the dealer count dropped by 45 percent, our revenue was flat for the year. Yes, we cancelled all direct marketing to reduce our acquisition costs to zero and lost 45 percent of the customer base that pays the bills, yet our revenue stayed flat for the year. The reason? Consumers coming from the traditional advertising channels dropped by 90 percent because we stopped advertising on TV. Yet the volume of car buyers coming in from our affinity channels—the flywheel—actually increased. The sustained volume and credible partnerships with USAA, American Express, *Consumer Reports*, and 100 other brands— our affinity channel—were too powerful to stop the business flywheel. That's why the 3,100 dealers that remained in the program actually saw increased sales per month, which is why TrueCar's overall revenue remained flat, even including the 90 percent loss from the consumer- direct channel.

BD not only increases sales but also softens the impact of a market downturn. Even if one revenue channel is cut off, revenue from other partnerships continues and can make up the shortfall or even surpass it.

As of this publishing date, our dealer customers are back up to 6,500, and *Automotive News* published an article on May 6, 2013, declaring "Affinity sales saved the day for TrueCar." Here's the first paragraph:

Automotive News

Affinity sales saved the day for TrueCar

Painter: When Web site traffic fell off, organization members kept buying

David Barkhoiz

Automotive News | May 6, 2013 – 12:01 am EST

TrueCar Inc. owes its survival to the 1,500 associations, including USAA and AAA, that give their members an opportunity to buy vehicles through the online auto-shopping service, TrueCar CEO Scott Painter said last week.

Those affinity groups are among TrueCar's oldest customers, and their members continued to buy cars last year through TrueCar, even after dealers abandoned TrueCar in droves and the company's Web site business plunged.

"Our affinity partners got us through," Painter said.

TrueCar is an online vehicle-buying site that allows dealers to offer discounted prices to customers who come to the site either via truecar.com or the many affinity groups offering the service. About 250,000 new and used vehicles were bought through TrueCar in 2012 with new-vehicle sales representing about 2 percent of U.S. vehicles sold.

THE SALES-ONLY APPROACH

Pursuing sales growth can help improve your top-line revenue in the short term, but long term, the business does not appreciably change. Your model, your growth strategy, and your tactics are the same; only the pace increases in order to ramp up sales figures. As the company grows, its ability to continue to achieve mid-double-digit growth declines; market saturation is a limiting factor. Eventually, sales of existing products and services will lag, only to increase again once you roll out a new product.

Groupon is a great example of this. They were *the* hot company for a while. Google offered them $6 billion in 2010, and they turned it down. Yet throughout their growth, they did not establish an effective sumo advantage. Instead, they crafted a blueprint for others to quickly emerge and compete. As the market became saturated with Groupon-like offers, Groupon took the majority of the hit. They were on their own. They were the first to create the "flash sale" platform, yet now there are too many companies that offer flash sales. So what was Groupon thinking? How did they plan to (a) sustain their growth and (b) create a competitive advantage? Perhaps they should have partnered to power Google, AOL, Walmart, Costco, or American Express.

Groupon did partner with Expedia for travel, so they do deserve credit for partnering with a sumo, but, in my view, they chose the wrong partner and the wrong vertical. Travel is not where they needed to establish a beachhead. Google signaled that they were going to enter the space. At that moment, Groupon's greatest vulnerability was with the local market presence they had spent time and money building. I don't know enough about the internal situation at Groupon, but I believe an executive with the right BD philosophy would have made sure that Groupon had a more stable future by developing a BD Layer with strategic advantages for the company and simultaneously making it harder for new competitors to enter the space. As I see it, Google and others entering the market were inevitable, so Groupon should have been thinking about how to compete with them shortly after launching the company.

Conversely, LivingSocial, a Groupon competitor, struck a deal with Amazon to power Amazon Local, their local deals program. Amazon made an investment, and, in turn, LivingSocial's sales force now sells ads for both LivingSocial and Amazon Local. Through that one deal, LivingSocial catapulted to Amazon-size status in the category. By buying 29 percent of the company, Amazon avoided the big tech build out and the distraction and resource drain in development of a local field sales force across the country by aligning with LivingSocial. LivingSocial, on the other hand, got Amazon's eyeballs, demographics, behavioral purchase data, and credibility in one fell swoop. I can't think of a better example of two companies working together for the benefit of both and their collective customers.

BD is a proven way to achieve accelerated growth. That is because BD is a game changer. BD efforts can completely transform a company's business model, strategy, and client base. It's not about selling more of an already-developed product or service to a waiting market. Instead, it's about recognizing a market opportunity, envisioning what a solution might look like, and then pursuing established partners to completely own that market.

Take Carfax, for example. The company achieved massive growth when they evolved their sale-centric philosophy to include a BD Layer. At Carfax, the partnership effort had always reported to the sales department. It was subservient to sales for the first 10 or 11 years of its existence. And, don't get me wrong, Carfax had experienced strong sales growth but nothing like what they achieved once BD was separated from sales.

Dick Raines, the president of Carfax, knew it was time to separate the BD function from sales when he recognized Carfax was not creating the strategic levers it should have in the marketplace. When the BD effort was pulled out from under sales and then replaced with BD people and managed with a BD philosophy, the company was able to identify new business opportunities and pursue them without the shackles of sales quotas or contracts. That new approach led to true accelerated growth.

Over the next two years, Carfax accomplished, on a strategic level, more than they did in the previous 11 years put together. The company experienced a new boost of revenue growth because the approach was strategic, not transaction focused. The BD effort was not at all concerned with closing a deal by the end of the current quarter. To the contrary, the team was focused on partnering with other companies that would catapult the business into an entirely different level of operation. Had BD remained under sales' control, revenue would have been far less than what Carfax obtained over the subsequent five years and continues to enjoy today. Again, BD is strategic. It should have long-lasting effects on the business.

THE WHOLE IS GREATER THAN THE SUM OF ITS PARTS

The reason BD can be transformational is that the whole is greater than the sum of its parts. You've probably heard that saying before, and nowhere is it more appropriate than in BD. BD is about taking the assets or capabilities of two or more companies and combining them to create a third, even more valuable asset. The sum of the partners' assets is much greater than the two separately. The same can't be said of pure sales figures—with sales, you add the sales of two companies together to get total revenue. It's simple math. But in BD, two companies working together to create a new product or service, or to serve an entirely different market, can achieve sales that are two, three, even 10 times what the two companies individually sold. There's a multiplier at work that can drive revenue up several times what it had been.

Depending on the size of the company, year-over-year (YOY) revenue growth should go from low double digit to high double digit or even triple digit with the proper BD effort. That's the impact that BD and the Sumo Advantage have on a company. But it takes time. BD deals take at least a three-year commitment to get from proposal to results. It can take one or two years just to get commitment on a deal and then another year of relationship management before you can assess how big an impact that deal is going to have for both partners. It's not something you try for six months and then bail on if it doesn't seem to be moving fast enough. The timetable for BD is much longer than for sales.

In sales, employees are incentivized to focus on their performance in the current quarter. What deals can they close in a matter of weeks? It's all about speed. Yet in BD, speed is generally your enemy. Pushing too hard to seal a deal can be its death.

SPOTTING THE DIFFERENCES

While speed is one of many differentiators between sales and BD, it is not one of the four major distinctions. The four distinctions between sales and BD are:

1. BD is strategic in nature, not transaction focused.
2. No direct revenue is generated when executing a BD contract, as it is with sales.
3. Key contacts have a full plate of tasks to attend to, and your proposed BD deal isn't on it.
4. Every sales book drives the importance of "getting to yes." But in BD, you don't focus on getting to a yes—you focus on not getting a no. This is critical with BD deals.

Understanding the distinctions can help you successfully land a deal, first off, and, later, manage it to ensure even greater success. The first three distinctions are statements of fact about the BD process and your target prospect; understanding the nature of the situation can help you overcome the obstacles that may be placed in your way. The fourth distinction is behavioral and a strategy for success in BD deals. Ignore the advice to "always be closing," as in sales, and aim only not to be shut down.

I. BD IS STRATEGIC.

BD is all about strategy, about identifying a need or opportunity in the marketplace and a partner who can give you an advantage in meeting that need. To conceive of a BD deal takes vision and a problem-solving nature, coupled with knowledge of the marketplace and the major players.

You'll need to paint a vivid picture of what the opportunity is: how working together with a sumo your two companies can take advantage of the opportunity and what the upside potential is. You're part storyteller and part inspirational leader as you begin testing the waters. When pitching a company, you don't just talk about making money. Instead, you seize ownership of how your vision will actually grow the sumo's business. Yes! You are so passionate about the possibilities that the sumo will soon look to you for help in their own arena.

Sales, on the other hand, is about selling something tangible or concrete in concept. It's about meeting an immediate need a company has for something. As I often say, it's about selling paper cups. There's really nothing strategic about it. As a paper cup sales rep, your job is to track down which companies need cups and then sell them as many as you can. Pretty straightforward. Sure, you may need to do a little digging to find the right procurement contact for paper products, but that's about the extent of your strategizing. Then it's primarily a numbers game. How many cups do they want, what specifications do they have, how many can you deliver, how quickly, and at what price? You focus on your quick objection responses and, hopefully, you get the order.

You wouldn't take a BD approach to selling paper cups because it simply isn't needed. Persuading a customer to purchase cups has more to do with product features, availability, delivery speed, and cost than anything else. So you don't need to try to get a meeting with senior management or build a relationship with your key contact over several

10

months, as you would with a BD deal. They don't need a vision of what life using your paper cups will be like; they just need you to make a deal with their procurement rep. It's a transaction, not a company-altering event.

2. THERE IS NO DIRECT REVENUE WITH BD DEALS.

According to the Merriam-Webster dictionary, the definition of sales is "the transfer of ownership of and title to property from one person to another for a price." In sales, you agree on sales terms, issue an invoice, and get a check in 30 to 45 days for the paper cups you just sold. In the meantime, you start working to sell cups to the next prospect on your list. The sales cycle is complete in a matter of days or weeks.

On a BD deal, you may sign a contract after taking more than a year to come to a meeting of the minds, but still no money changes hands. Not one dollar. All the work that needs to be done to generate revenue *begins* at that point, and the fruits of that labor will come months later. Even then, you don't know exactly how much money will be generated.

But unlike sales, where shaving some money off your price quote may make the difference between getting the contract or not, in BD, there are no price quotes or purchase orders. Sure, the money you and your partner can make together is what drives the deal, but it's never as cut-and-dried as in sales. You're collaborating in the hopes that one day in the near future you'll be able to sell another entity on what you've developed jointly, whether it's a product or service, technology, or capability. However, when the contract is signed, you don't earn any money—only the potential to make money down the road. That's a second major distinction between BD and sales.

3. YOUR BD PROSPECTS ALREADY HAVE A FULL PLATE.

Everyone's busy—that's true whether you're in sales or BD. However, when you're in sales and you have a product or service a company needs, the responsibility to buy it is already on your customer's plate. You don't need to convince your client at Starbucks or McDonald's that they need cups; they already know that. In fact, your sales prospect will need to take action at some point to be sure their company doesn't run out of paper cups. Those cups are on their plate of job responsibilities.

Your proposed BD deal, which may be a solution to changes emerging in their industry, or something similar, is not. It's not on their plate, not on their boss's plate, not on the company's plate—not even in their consciousness. No one in their entire decision-making process cares at all about partnering with you at the moment. Because they are not going to be compensated for considering all the "what-ifs" of their industry. In the beginning, there is only downside to taking time to consider your proposal. This is because it means adding more to their already overloaded plate, and stuff that is already on the plate now becomes at risk of falling off or being forgotten or delayed.

Most BD deals address market opportunities that many companies don't realize exist. That's a hard sell. First you have to make them aware of the current situation, impress upon them the opportunity they have, and then convince them that you're the best partner to pursue that opportunity—all when they really had other, more pressing concerns on their plate for today. Getting a prospect's attention is so much harder in a BD deal than in sales, not to mention getting them to acknowledge that your idea has merit. That's why such deals can take months or years to bring to fruition.

The truth is that there's only risk, and no reward, from your prospect's perspective. And the reward won't likely come for years. They have so little incentive to give you any of their time. Their plate is already full, which is why the method in which you approach BD deals is critical.

4. IN BD DEALS, AIM FOR NOT GETTING A NO.

One of my favorite movie scenes is Alec Baldwin's "motivational" speech in the movie *Glengarry Glen Ross*. He motivates the sales team by telling them that they are all fired but that they each have one week to regain their jobs starting with "tonight's sit." Baldwin reminds them of the ABC's of sales—**A**lways **B**e **C**losing! In sales, you're taught to always be closing. Your sole goal is to get a yes from your potential customer. To do that, you lead them down that slippery slope of yeses to close the deal—the deal that will immediately generate a commission for you. As a salesperson, you want to get that yes.

Not so in BD. In BD, you have no chance in hell of getting a yes at the outset. For all the reasons we've just covered, you're not getting a yes. Give up on it. Your potential partner doesn't know who you are, doesn't know why you're bugging them, certainly doesn't want to add anything else to their already long to-do list, and doesn't want to risk screwing up on the work that they've already been tasked with. So don't even think about trying to get a yes from them on your first series of meetings. It's not happening. Worse, pushing too hard could make it more difficult for you to close the deal in the future. So don't go for a yes.

As Baldwin yelled to the sales team in the movie, Mitch and Murray offered the winner of the sales contest a Cadillac Eldorado. That's about getting to a yes as fast as you can. While your BD people should not use sales techniques to close, as the CEO of your company or leader of your team, don't use sales motivation techniques, either. Sales contests and quarterly bonuses won't mean a thing.

On the other hand, you really don't want to hear no, either. In fact, it is your job to ensure you don't get a no. To keep the ball rolling forward, keep sharing intriguing but "limited" information, developing a relationship with your key contact, and trying to maintain control of the process, without getting cut off. You don't want to be prevented from getting an initial meeting—or a second meeting—with decision makers, nor do you want to be told outright by the CEO that the company has no interest in your plans.

While you can often sidestep a no by turning to other players within the company, that takes extra work. Better to stick with your current contact and keep moving the deal forward without being given an outright no. Keep focusing on educating and informing your prospect until you finally get that "aha" moment, that moment of clarity when your prospect sees the potential of what you're proposing. Then, and only then, do you start working on getting a yes, which is the complete opposite of how sales approaches the process.

GETTING PAST NO

I'm betting that the first time Nike approached Apple about working together on a running shoe, the execs at Apple might have scratched their heads a little. "What the hell does Apple know about running shoes?" they may have asked themselves. And the truth is that Apple probably knew next to nothing. But someone within Nike had a vision of a running shoe that could be linked to an Apple device, such as an iPod, to not only play music but also collect fitness data. A partnership between Nike, the number-one shoe manufacturer in the world, and Apple, known for its technology innovation, to design, develop, and introduce such a shoe made a lot of sense from a business development point of view. And that's how the whole BD process began in the mid-2000s.

Nike approached Apple, and while it's highly likely that Apple had previously never given a moment's thought to developing an Apple-compatible running shoe, the more information Nike shared about their product goals, the fewer nos they heard. In the end, the companies collaborated to create the Nike+iPod, an iPod-compatible running shoe that tracks information on time, distance, calories burned, and pace and stores it on the iPod using a built-in shoe sensor that Apple provides. The shoe was introduced in 2006.

However, that BD deal did require that Nike say no to other partners, such as Android. In fact, it took six more years before the Android version of the Nike+ app was released, in 2012, long after Apple had established the market. Apple also said no to Nike's competition.

The BD deal, the partnership, between Apple and Nike was strategic for both. It took time to define and finalize, and it ultimately created new income streams for both: Nike developed a new running product using a sensor that Apple sold them, and Apple cornered the market temporarily for real-time personal running data captured on their product. It was a one-two punch by these market makers, born out of a BD proposal.

CATEGORY AWARENESS IS THE GREAT SEPARATOR

Nearly all BD deals start where there is no category awareness. Was Apple thinking about footwear and apparel development before Nike approached them? Highly unlikely. Likewise, the company you're pitching may be thinking about advertising, or customer relationship management (CRM), or security but not about food service, or property management, or automotive fleet management, or anything you're pitching. It's not on their radar. But if that's where the opportunity lies that you want to pursue, it's your job to *make* them aware and to help them visualize what's possible. You propose a strategic partnership to develop and pursue this jointly. That's BD.

But if the company has been thinking about security, for example, it's on someone's plate. It's someone's responsibility. That individual needs to, at some point, investigate how to increase security for the company and their employees. So when you approach them about a new tool—a key fob, let's say—that generates a constantly rotating password that employees would use to access highly sensitive company information, they're sold. It's exactly in line with what they were looking for. Granted, they weren't aware of this type of product or its functionality before you called, but they knew they were after a security solution. You pitch it, they love the product, they're sold. And in the end, there is nothing strategic about this deal. You made a sale. They cut you a check. You move on to your next prospect. That's sales.

That's also very different from approaching a company about jointly developing an entirely new security system that does not currently exist, rather than selling an off-the-shelf product. Maybe this new security system utilizes biometric sensing technology to determine identity and verify access and behavior through an independent database. It may even leverage geolocation using technology exclusive to wireless carriers. This type of new system requires expertise in security, as well as biotech, possibly with multiple wireless carriers. Developing this new technology jointly versus going it alone could occur only through a BD deal, as evidenced by the four distinctions: (1) because developing such a technology and product would be a strategic decision for both companies, (2) no revenue would be generated on the front end, (3) it is not clear initially who within the target company would be responsible for championing such an initiative, and (4) going for the yes initially will only get the project shot down.

USING THE FOUR DISTINCTIONS

Understanding that sales and BD are two separate and distinct processes is fairly easy, but recognizing when one approach should be used over another can get tricky. The Four Distinctions are four questions, essentially, to help you determine what type of deal you're looking at and how it should best be approached. You shouldn't send a professional salesperson out to close a BD deal that is two or three years away from being finalized, just as you shouldn't send a BD pro out to sell paper cups or security key chains. Their skill sets are different and, when misapplied, inefficient.

However, sales is still a key ingredient in BD success. Your sales team consists of the people who benefit the most from the BD Layer. For example, when TrueCar approached a large insurance and financial services company focusing on military and their families (let's call them "Big Sumo 1") about partnering to boost its auto loan business, BD made the pitch, communicated the picture of what could be, and finalized the terms of the deal. But it was the dealer sales team that came in and built the network of dealers to service Big Sumo 1 members who were buying a new car. They were the ones making calls, setting up meetings, and putting into place the dealer network that was essential to the success of the project as a whole. The deal with Big Sumo 1 made the sales pitch to auto dealers much more compelling and accelerated the growth of the dealer network. Each team has its role, which is different and distinct, but both are important for success.

I'm not saying that a salesperson can't close a BD deal or that a BD exec can't sell. What I am saying is that you'll be more successful when you match the professional to the type of deal in front of you. The Four Distinctions can help you make that call.

THE BD LAYER—
YOUR COMPANY'S
TURBOCHARGER

Business development, or BD as I generally refer to it, has the potential to transform your company and turn the industry you serve upside down. It is a powerful tool that can put your company on an exponential growth curve. I like to say that it is a turbocharger that can be attached to your company's engine—your product development function—to produce even greater results. It's what most companies strive for.

Likewise, I define the Sumo Advantage as an entrepreneur's alignment with a major market force, capability, or accelerator with the intent to grow market share and crush the competition. The sumo fuels the turbocharger, providing power. The more power it has, the faster the turbocharger works.

On an organizational chart, the BD Layer sits between the product development and sales and marketing functions. While BD impacts all areas within a company, it affects these two the most. However, the degree to which you partner with a sumo, or the amount of fuel you have to power your turbocharger, will determine the results your company sees from its relationships. Strategic partnerships are rooted at the product layer to jointly build a new solution but accelerate at the sales and marketing layer through the connection with each respective customer.

Once the connection between BD and the product layer is galvanized, the turbocharging begins to take effect. There is an immediate impact on the market, starting with your first communication. There is a big difference, from your competitors' perspective at least, between issuing a press release announcing that your company has released a new technology to help solve problem X and an announcement that your company and IBM or Apple or Google have partnered to solve the problem. The existence of a sumo partner increases your likelihood of success in the eyes of the outside world, which is what causes a market shift. You are taken much more seriously, thanks to your sumo.

However, there are partnerships and there are partnerships.

PROMOTIONAL PARTNERSHIPS ARE NOT BD

BD partnerships are distinctively different from purely promotional, or sales, partnerships. BD partnerships generate no direct revenue; they are strategic, not transactional; your target clients have not thought about how a partnership with your company could benefit them; and to succeed, you need to focus more on not getting a no than on getting a yes, as you would in sales. Yet some companies get confused about what, exactly, a partnership entails.

BD partnerships involve leveraging the product development and the sales and marketing layers of both companies, with the BD Layer in between fueling the venture. But there is no BD Layer if your company simply creates a promotional partnership with another company, where the two of you work in parallel, rather than collectively.

Promotional partnerships involve two or more companies that agree to promote the others' products or services to their mutual customer bases. In many cases the exchange results in revenue in the form of a referral fee or affiliate commission. For example, if Delta Airlines e-mailed its customer base offering a discount the next time they rented a car with Enterprise and Enterprise e-mailed its customers with a promotional code for their next airline reservation on Delta, the two companies are promoting each other. Are they partners? Sort of, but not in any strategic way. When Delta's customers rent with Enterprise, they'll receive an affiliate commission; likewise for Enterprise when their customers make a reservation with Delta. They are cross promoting. But the revenue generated is not substantial, it doesn't impact either company's operations, and it certainly doesn't shift the market—it's just a legal sales kickback, really. It's not a BD deal.

Even if such partnerships generate revenue for both businesses, if no product development capabilities are tapped and the market has not shifted, we're not talking about BD. It is simply a sales and marketing arrangement that does not involve the product or BD Layer. It is a stand-alone event with little impact.

INTEGRATION IS THE CORNERSTONE OF BD PARTNERSHIPS

In contrast, when you integrate your sumo's capabilities with your own company's core competencies, you are creating a turbocharger that will generate significant revenues for both companies. That alignment of core products that involves both product and sales and marketing layers has the potential to radically shake up your industry. That's the effect you're after.

Starting at the product layer, your BD partnerships include how, when, and why products are developed. The sumo you've partnered with has unique advantages—aspects that have made them a superior warrior in their own space. Your challenge is now to apply those same advantages to your market so you can crush your competition.

What this means is linking the product development and sales and marketing activities *of both companies* to create a new solution. The product layer is where all product development occurs. When you're working with a sumo, you will want to incorporate some of the advantages their product or service provides, which comes from their organization's product layer. That integration is key.

Through integration, the product itself changes. No longer are you selling your product or their product—you're selling a modified, changed, improved product based on the two companies' advantages. You don't just want your product or service to be a benefit. It needs to align with their core product. That's where product changes occur that fire up the turbocharger.

MAKING WAVES IN THE MARKET

Even sumos in their own right can still need a sumo. Redbox could announce live streaming, and Netflix could take note. But partnering with Verizon garners a higher level of attention.

Announcing on its own is unlikely to capture much attention these days. It might be interesting, but it's less meaningful. It's not just you saying, "I'm going to do this." Smaller companies have an even harder time. Partnerships and joint ventures are so commonplace that they cause barely a ripple in the market when announced. When Redbox announced that they wanted to get into online streaming to compete with Netflix, Amazon, and Hulu, few companies seemed to care. No one really took them seriously. But when they announced they had partnered with Verizon and would be streaming movies on the Verizon network, you'd better believe Netflix, Amazon, and Hulu sat up and took notice. This was a game changer.

That's what a BD deal does. It shifts the dynamic in the market. The same could be said about Barnes & Noble and Microsoft's "strategic partnership," which was announced in 2012. Barnes & Noble's NOOK e-reader has been an also ran since its development and release in 2009. The Android-based reader competes primarily with the Amazon Kindle, the Apple iPad, and the Kobo e-reader and had been making some headway in attracting buyers with each iteration of its product. But when it announced its partnership with Microsoft, suddenly the market dynamic shifted. No longer could the NOOK be considered the "distant second" player with no chance of catching up. By leveraging Microsoft's financial resources, which included a $300 million investment in the venture, as well as its software capabilities to release a NOOK for the Windows 8 platform, Barnes & Noble could quickly broaden their product's appeal.

The chances of success with these two companies are much greater. The two together can deal with how to serve the education market. Barnes & Noble doesn't have the power to transform the university system into a completely paperless environment, even though the company may control content distribution on many campuses through their campus bookstore operation. That's where Microsoft helps.

In fact, the partnership's stated goal is to "accelerate the transition to e-reading," with particular emphasis on the education market, where Barnes & Noble has a foothold with their more than 600 college bookstores. By converting college students to e-reader usage for textbooks and other reading, the two companies may be hoping to mimic Apple's original strategy of pursuing product adoption at the college level. Amazon must take notice now of Barnes & Noble, versus having announced on their own that they were trying to advance the digital reading market. Now Amazon has to respond to this partnership in a very different way. Again, the market has shifted with this pairing.

Another recent example of a turbocharged partnership is Babies "R" Us and Whattoexpect.com. Babies "R" Us is clearly the sumo in this relationship, but Whattoexpect brings value, too. Babies "R" Us has the mammoth retail operation, and Whattoexpect has the pregnancy expertise and scads of content. By integrating Whattoexpect's content and customer base with the Babies "R" Us registry, which is now accessible on Whattoexpect.com, the partners can potentially own this market segment. So while BuyBuyBaby or USABaby might have previously ignored news about Whattoexpect, especially since they have only an online presence, the alliance with Babies "R" Us puts them in a whole new category and shakes up the market for baby gear.

LockerDome and USA Today Sports Digital Properties is another example. LockerDome is the relative newcomer in sports social media publishing, but they have already amassed an eight-million-a-month unique visitor base and are likely to go after Yahoo! Sports. But LockerDome and USA Today Sports together are a different type of threat to Yahoo! Sports. "Sports enthusiasts join LockerDome to become a part of interest-specific sports communities where they can consume content and interact with like-minded fans around their favorite professional athletes, teams and sports," reports a recent press release. The site is growing at a rate of approximately 100,000 new and unique visitors a day. Those numbers were presumably appealing to *USA Today*, which agreed to begin selling ads on LockerDome, while LockerDome's content will begin appearing within the USA Today Sports Digital Properties' network.

By integrating each other's back-end systems, to enable ads to be sold and content to be shared, the two companies are positioning themselves for exponential growth. This partnership is much more than a simple cross promotion.

THROWING THE SUMO'S WEIGHT AROUND

The BD Layer forces velocity through the sales effort. Your teams should close more transactions at a faster pace, which lowers cost and increases revenue at an accelerated rate. The BD Layer is your revenue turbocharger.

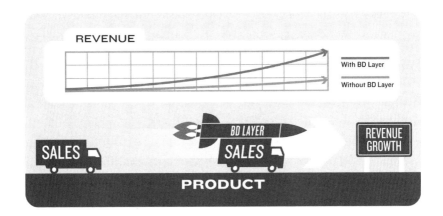

BASKING IN THE TRUST AURA

Your sumo can also help overcome customer objections, among other things. Think about the objections you hear today regarding why a prospect does not buy from you. Is it scalability? Long-term risk? Or maybe the lack of data, which could be more easily accessed through the sumo? A sumo's weight helps with many objections or concerns. You are much more credible through the halo effect of your sumo's brand. If you are gaining access to customers that have already chosen your sumo, then you know several things about them:

- They are buyers/customers/users.
- They trust the sumo as a provider.
- They utilize the sumo today to solve a problem or satisfy a desire.
- They are more inclined to say yes than your typical customers because of the sumo.

The key concept to understand with the BD Layer is that it exists when entrepreneurs and sumos truly partner, leveraging the core competencies of both companies and integrating them to develop an entirely new product or process. It comes into being with that product integration. Without any true integration, the BD Layer is nonexistent. The product layer and sales and marketing layers still function but only in parallel.

PART II

HOW YOU GET A DEAL

3

FINDING YOUR SUMO

Now that you understand how business development can accelerate sales growth in your company and you recognize the importance of partnering with sumos to leapfrog your competition, what do you do first?

Answer the following two questions:

1. For those audiences generating direct revenue, what are the top five reasons why they choose (a) you over the competitor or (b) a competitor over your services?
2. What unique assets (behavioral or technical) can influence each audience to increase the value of the products or services that you provide?

With all of that in mind, you need a literal and intuitive feeling of what your assets look like. It's not just about your company but also the companies that you are connected to and, in this case, that are already paying you money (or not).

Here's an example of some unique assets. TrueCar has partnerships with strong national brands such as USAA and Consumer Reports. Those brands have extremely loyal members. That's an asset. Another asset dealing with the same group is that not everyone can become a member of each of these brands. Can anyone become an American Express Platinum cardholder or a member of the National Education Association?

Now, start to think about what could be done with your assets. Think about where you want to go and what you need to get there. Think about how you can crush your competition. What would be a serious blow to them? What would make them take you more seriously? How do you become more relevant in your space? How do you ensure no one can knock you out?

Look at your list of assets as if they were organized on a chessboard. Each of your assets is a playing piece of sorts. So how do you collect more assets? You may find a common theme among your customers or, more importantly, among their customers or assets. It could be something that is missing—an integration point that they may need or that you can bring to them.

For example, many small businesses rely on a referral network. If you have a network of insurance agents that refers business to you, think about how to make those partnerships (asset) deeper. Try to move your relationship with those referral agents from a "nice to have" status to a "want to have" status. Your goal should be to make the agents better for their customers. Perhaps you can build some technical integration between the referral systems and your systems.

Your goal is to establish a connection so the agent is not just making a referral but also actually providing a higher level of service to his or her customers that other agents may not be. Referrals are nice, but having your referral network feel that your solution is part of their solution is better.

Is there a Sumo of software systems that dominates the insurance agent industry? Perhaps it is very fragmented and you have to establish many partnerships. The key is to find out how this process occurs and what it will take to get an integration partnership to move you from a "nice to have" to a "need to have."

Finding your sumo is not a simple exercise. When talking to CEOs, I have found many that find this to be a difficult process. The idea of thinking so out of the box for an effort that has nothing to do with the company's day-to-day blocking and tackling or hitting the quarterly or annual numbers is a serious challenge. When this happens, I suggest an alternative approach.

Get the thought leaders of your company in a room with a whiteboard and start discussing how you can get hurt. Play the "What if?" game. Start thinking about: "What if your competitor did X?" "What if your competitor got a deal with a key sumo?" "What could your competitor do that would box you out of the market?" "What would you do to try to minimize the impact?"

Rather than first thinking about the myriad approaches you *could* take to crush your competition, where the sky's the limit, first think about what your competition could do that would be disastrous to you. Go into reactive mode. What would that look like? Whom would it involve? This is what I call Path One. It's your first line of thinking.

Evaluate how your competitor's potential actions could negatively impact you. Ask yourself, "How would that hurt my business?" If they steal market share, if they steal a partner, if they get a certain capability that your customers are asking for by building it or partnering with a company that already has it—what does that mean for you? How do you counteract such a move by a major competitor? What countermeasures should you be prepared to take?

Brainstorm worst-case scenarios as a starting point for identifying the partners that you should be focusing on.

BLOCKBUSTER'S INABILITY TO ADAPT PROVES DEADLY

Had Blockbuster taken this approach, they might still be a category leader. Instead of studying the market and paying attention to the speed at which new technology, such as streaming video, was being adopted, they were more worried about Redbox's move into their industry. They weren't studying the big picture and developing strategies to counteract their potential worst-case scenario.

Blockbuster had a nationwide presence and millions of customers accustomed to driving to their stores to pay $5 a night to rent a new-release movie. Then Redbox came along, with their self-service kiosks and $1 price tag, and Blockbuster got nervous. So they dropped their price to match Redbox's and soon after went into bankruptcy in 2010, because their lower revenue couldn't support the company's massive overhead. Unfortunately, Redbox wasn't their biggest problem. Netflix and other live-streaming video companies were. But they didn't see it coming. Netflix sealed Blockbuster's fate when it began offering DVDs by mail, without late fees, for rates lower than Blockbuster was charging.

What's interesting is that Redbox and Verizon have now partnered to compete with Netflix. While Amazon has decided to go head-to-head with Netflix for streaming, Redbox Instant is offering both DVDs and streaming to get ahead of the largest sumo in the ring. They changed the value proposition, and now Netflix is a little more vulnerable. Redbox doesn't yet have the content, but with Verizon behind them, they have a better shot of getting there, and, if so, subscribers will have the benefit of streaming and DVD pickup for the same price as the monthly Netflix streaming subscription fee.

Aligning with Redbox is a killer move, and Netflix may not have seen that coming.

THE PROACTIVE STRATEGY

Now look at the flip side, Path Two. Once you've looked at the market from a reactive perspective, look at it from a proactive standpoint. How do you prevent some of those disastrous situations from occurring? By going on the offensive. Forget about what your competitors could do, and now think about what you could do to them. What sumo should you approach to fortify your company? What deal would solidify a market leader position? What moves can you make that will have your competitors crying "uncle"?

Path Two is thinking about how to leapfrog your competition in your space. It's the opposite of Path One. But then you have to really consider how to make it work from an integrated standpoint. Your goal is to get the market to converge on your business.

That's where you start in your own BD efforts.

P&G AND WALMART

That thought process may be the reason that Procter & Gamble (P&G) partnered with Walmart several years ago. The consumer goods powerhouse and the logistics sumo together look unstoppable. Where P&G offers product manufacturing of more than 83 brands, Walmart has distribution capabilities second to none. Some of P&G's top-selling brands include Tide laundry detergent, Folgers coffee, Ivory soap, and Bounty paper towels. Walmart is the largest company in the world. So it makes sense that these two sumo powerhouses would want to join forces.

P&G and Walmart have a well-established channel partnership, where both companies share data about customers and products. Knowing exactly what customers want benefits both Walmart, which can be more efficient in its inventory management, and P&G, which

35

can use data collected by Walmart to develop new products that meet stated customer demand. Linking both companies' sales data allows them to drive down costs of production and distribution, increasing profits for both companies. The two sumos, together, are nearly impossible to beat. Who's your Walmart, and how can you turn your largest customer into your sumo partner?

LEVERAGE DOMINANCE

In 2011, one of Staples' marketing executives took a new position as chief marketing officer at online print house Vistaprint, following reports of growing demand for business cards. Interestingly, Vistaprint sells more business cards than anything else in their inventory. They are typically the low-price leader on most fronts, but what they lack is speed. If you place an order today at Vistaprint and need your business cards later this week, you may pay close to $25 in rush charges to get them in time.

Over at Staples, customers can have their business cards printed in a matter of hours, but until recently, they had to choose from a limited selection of templates, have the cards designed by an independent designer, or place an order online through Staples, which offered a skinned version of Vistaprint designs; that is, the designs available online at Staples.com were the exact same ones Vistaprint offers. However, placing an order online then required the same wait times as those at Vistaprint.

Fast-forward to 2013 and Vistaprint and Staples announced a partnership that allows Vistaprint customers to design their business cards at the company's website, but instead of having them shipped, they can specify Staples as the pickup location, where the cards can be ready in fewer than four hours. This BD deal, which gives Vistaprint a way to compete with local quick-print businesses, also boosts Staples' business by leveraging their printing equipment and giving customers another reason to come into the store.

Vistaprint has the design capabilities, and Staples has the on-site printing equipment and brick-and-mortar locations. Together they can likely dominate the business card printing business.

That is a smart strategic deal to make and one that OfficeDepot/OfficeMax and FedEx should have been considering. But OfficeMax and OfficeDepot were working on a merger at the time to try to gain market share from Staples and probably weren't thinking about other partners.

WHERE TO BEGIN

After assessing who your biggest sumo allies could be, your next step is agreeing that you're open for partnership. You may even want to have this discussion before your in-house brainstorming session. Your culture has to change to adopt this type of move. There's never a situation where there are no deals to do. There are always deals to do. If you can't spot them, you're just not thinking.

The reason that being open to commitment is key is that you're going to have to allocate some resources to be successful in BD. That starts with the right individuals to go out and hunt for deals and follows with a commitment that if they land a sumo, you're going to be willing to provide support, both to your BD pros and to the sumo they bring to the table. You have to support the sumo, too.

Depending on the size of your company, that initial BD person is most likely the CEO. He or she is the most qualified to discuss partnerships and communicate confidence to potential partners. He or she is also in the best position to communicate passion and vision. Remember that these are evangelic pitches. You're not selling paper cups.

Then you have to understand the differences between pursuing a sales relationship and pursuing a BD relationship. It boils down to the four distinctions:

1. BD is strategic in nature, not transaction focused.
2. No direct revenue is generated when executing a BD contract, as it is in sales.
3. Key contacts have a full plate of tasks to attend to, and your proposed BD deal isn't on it.
4. Focusing on not getting a no, versus getting a yes, is critical to closing BD deals.

The CEO of your company needs to lead the discussion, setting the stage for a BD mind-set. That means making it clear that resources will be provided to support BD initiatives. Once that is clear, you can begin identifying potential partners, followed quickly by identifying the best person internally to reach out to. It might be the CEO who makes a call to the potential partner CEO. Or your head of BD calls that company's head of product development—whoever you think is a good starting point.

If it is unclear who the best point person might be to contact at your target sumo organization, I, personally, start reading online press releases. I look for information about the company, its partners, and other deals they've done. I look to see who is quoted in the press release. I use Google to find out whether senior executives have said things in speeches, presentations, or press releases that trigger an alignment between what they're stating and what you would like to do with them. Try to find a hook and their motivation for talking with you.

Once you've confirmed that the company's goals may be in alignment with your partnership opportunity, reach out to the person who seems to be in charge of a business unit or function that matches with your idea. The best-case scenario is that someone on your team knows someone within the company, but in most situations, you'll be cold-calling.

YOUR PITCH

Keep in mind that as you start approaching potential partners, your concept has to be fairly developed. You can't call a sumo and suggest, "It would be great if we could sit in a room and brainstorm how we might work together." Uh, no. They don't have time to waste brainstorming. You've got to convince that sumo to get in the ring with you, on your side. To do that you need to have a pretty compelling vision.

Your idea, your vision, also needs to be recognized immediately as a no-brainer. For example, let's say you want to partner with the fruit grower Dole. So you call the VP of operations and say, "I'd like to partner with you to develop an irrigation system that won't break, won't get clogged, and uses half the amount of water you need to keep crops growing at an optimal rate. We have the technology and need a major partner." Where's the downside in that pitch? There isn't one. I'd be shocked if you got a no, because the benefits are so obvious. Then, together, you begin marketing it to Dole growers, as well as major farm operations worldwide. Dole gives you the stature in the industry to be taken seriously, and you have the system almost completely developed.

Remember that during these first conversations you're not trying to get anyone to sign a contract or even a nondisclosure agreement (NDA). You just want to have a deeper discussion about your plans. That's all. You're not going for a yes; you simply don't want to get a no.

So, at some point in the initial discussion, if it were me, I would say something to the effect of, "Hey, we're going to dominate in this area, and we want to find out whether you want to be involved in this." When they ask what you mean, you describe the state of the marketplace after the partnership. That might mean grabbing market share from a major competitor, getting out ahead of another, or developing a capability that nobody has yet.

If pushed for specifics, you might say something like, "I can't get into specifics until we get an NDA, but here's what I think we can accomplish together." It's an evangelical, high-level pitch. You give a few details to establish your credibility in the space but keep going back to what's possible. "If we can do A, that means that X, Y, and Z will be easy and lucrative," you say.

You don't have to have all the details worked out. If the sumo starts asking granular questions, then your answer can be, "Well, that depends. We'd need to learn more about your capabilities and long-term goals to understand exactly how it's going to work. But here's how I would envision the customer experience." Sure, you have no idea how you're going to get there, but you can paint a picture of the outcome—the target. You don't know the actual steps for integration, you don't know what platform they're on, and there's a whole slew of things you don't know, so don't go there. Keep it big picture.

As you're describing that big picture, be confident in your vision. Let your sumo know that "in the end, this is going to happen, whether it's with you or your major competitor. We *are* going to do this. We've done it before."

SPINNING YOUR STORY

Entrepreneurs are some of the most creative people on the planet. Not only can they spot opportunities and formulate strategies quickly but also they can present information in the most favorable light possible. They're like public relations ninjas in that regard. There's no bad news when you're talking to an entrepreneur.

For example, when asked about your experience in an industry, you may have none whatsoever, but your executives may have many years, so you talk about them. This might be stated as, "Three of the founders of the company have spent the past 20 years innovating in this particular space." Or, when asked about how secure your technology is, you might reference another sumo: "Well, we've worked with several financial institutions, and they are highly regulated by the Sarbanes-Oxley Act (SOX) and have significant personally identifiable information (PII) concerns, so I'm supremely confident it will pass yours." Flip any situation, such as the fact that you have no intention of integrating into their systems for PII, into an opportunity to talk about your big customers or partners and how well you perform. The key is to instill confidence that your company is going to succeed at your next strategic initiative.

NOT ALL DEALS ARE GOOD DEALS

As you're getting started in BD, you may be eager to sign your first sumo. Maybe you even feel some pressure to succeed. That pressure is good and will propel you to success, but don't get so focused on sealing a deal that you'll do anything to make it a reality. Sometimes the best decision is to turn down a deal.

I walked away from a really big sumo early in TrueCar's history. The other company was insisting that they co-own our intellectual property (IP) as we built out our business. That was an overreaching request and was completely unnecessary. It was ego driven, and this large insurance company thought that they could own us simply by agreeing to work with us. These deals are never worth it, yet it can be very hard for an entrepreneur to walk away from such a large opportunity. However, if the deal is unfair, you *must* walk away. Fast. It's not worth it and will ultimately ensure misalignment in the partnership, and from there, it all breaks down. If the deal is unfair at the outset, it's only going to get more unfair, not less.

BD can accelerate your sales, creating a springboard effect that vaults your sales into higher and higher levels. Once you identify and partner with a sumo that knows how you fight, knows how you think, and recognizes your strengths and your weaknesses, you'll be unstoppable. Landing that sumo is the first step, and once you've actually started partnering and collaborating, the sky is the limit as far as your sales are concerned.

I've seen it happen.

4

GAINING AND MAINTAINING CONTROL—A MUST

We've heard for years that in sales, the customer is always right. For me, this translates into, "The customer is always in control." In most cases, that's true. Customers control the money; therefore, they control the process. They determine exactly what they need, how many, when, and what their budget is and then decide which vendors are worthy of their business. Salespeople then compete for the business. By its nature, sales is reactive.

Business development is proactive. You're not responding to a need someone else has expressed. You're presenting an entirely new way of approaching a market opportunity. You're offering a proposal for someone else to respond to. And because you have the vision, the idea, for what your company could do when given access to a potential partner's resources, reputation, and customer base, you may think you are in control—at least for that initial moment, anyway. But since your entire vision depends on a deal with at least one of the sumos on your target list of two or possibly three, you really don't have any control. What you have is conviction—a belief that entrepreneurial spirit is going to get a deal closed. Your challenge is gaining and then maintaining control while keeping the process moving forward until you finalize an agreement and ultimately reap the rewards.

Your potential partner is, at first, in a "reactive" mode of control, reacting to your requests for a phone conversation or a meeting. They have the control because they decide whether they meet with you. They're reactive because they are not actively pursuing you or the idea. At any point, you can choose to take your vision to their competitor, but if they feel no concern for that, then you have not done your job yet. You are in control of the possibilities, and you want to let them know that. This is your first step in gaining some control. It's a process that gets harder and harder as your target sees the light. And as they begin to realize the size and impact of the initiative you are pitching, reactive control mode fades away. Suddenly, they "will get back to you" after thinking about it some more or after talking with others. As their interest rises, so does their subconscious desire for control. Instead of being reactive, they're now proactive. And once they decide they want in, another shift happens, and suddenly it's all about their terms. You can't let that happen. Success in BD depends on your maintaining control.

MOVING TOWARD A YES WITHOUT GETTING A NO

At the heart of that tussle for control is information. Whoever controls the information controls the process, in many cases. This means you need to fight to shape the conversations that are occurring, to direct the vision being shared, and to lead internal champions where you want to go based on the facts and figures you do and don't share. To do that, you need to carefully lead the pitch process along.

In BD, patience is king. While sales succeeds when the customer is rushed to close a deal, BD succeeds when the potential partner is eased gently along the path toward agreement. Slowly. Speed kills BD deals, so the last thing you want to do early in the game is try to get a commitment of any sort from any of your contacts. It's not time for that. In BD, you don't want to push for a yes early on. You merely don't want to hear no. That's your goal—not getting a no.

Think about a police negotiator talking with a suicidal person who is standing on the roof of a 10-story building. The negotiator's protocol is not to walk up on the roof and say, "Hey, get down from there now!" That's going for a yes but is more likely to result in a no or, in this case, a jump off the roof. The negotiator artfully inquires and presents information while simultaneously building a relationship and, consequently, keeping the person on the roof during the process. The negotiator is making sure he or she does not get a no by not yet asking for a yes.

At some point during the discussion, something changes in the dynamic. Perhaps the individual starts asking questions or tries to identify with the negotiator. "You've lost your job and your whole family was living in a shelter, too?" When that change occurs, it's time to go for a yes. The negotiator may say, "Let's get down off the roof and go grab a cup of coffee."

In sales, there are ways to hasten the deal's closing. You can offer incentives to shorten the sales cycle and get a yes more quickly when you're selling. You can set fictional deadlines to prompt a yes sooner or faster in sales. You can find many ways to sweeten the deal in sales but not so much in BD. When pitching an idea to a potential partner, there is little or no awareness of your company and the concept you're proposing, so setting a deadline will do nothing for you. You'll only get a no faster.

Let's face it: the odds of getting close to a yes are fairly low because three of the four distinctions between sales and BD are roadblocks:

(1) your proposal is not on your target contact's plate; (2) there is only indirect revenue associated with what you're proposing, not immediate and direct revenue; and (3) to keep the potential project alive, you need to avoid the no. And yet, from your contact's perspective, it's so much easier to say no to you. Everyone is empowered to say no. There are actually very few people in an organization who are empowered to say yes to you. But more importantly, there aren't many reasons to say yes, because yes means more work. There is a definite disincentive for your prospects to say yes.

Some nos are more serious than others, however. When you're starting the pitch process and trying to identify the right person to deal with, expect to get a lot of nos. That's a temporary no, like a wrong turn on a street, where you can quickly turn around. You cold-call, you ask questions, you get referred to someone else because the person you're speaking with isn't the right contact. That's OK. You're really just gathering information at this point, and the nos you hear only serve to point you toward a more appropriate contact within the company. You're zeroing in on the person who has the interest to say yes.

Notice how I did not say "the power to say yes." This is a strategic deal, and these types of decisions happen at an executive team level, not an individual level. Even the CEO, who clearly has the power to say yes, won't deliver a true yes without buy-in from his or her team. This brings up an important point, which we will get into later: whatever you do, avoid the top-down yes.

But also keep in mind that in the context of not getting a no while trying to gain and then maintain control, remember that you do need to be tenacious as hell. Persistence is key here as you start banging on doors.

OFFER INFORMATION
TO HOLD ATTENTION

Once you track down your actual prospect—the person you should be talking to—you need to obtain and maintain control over the call. The best way to do that is to start sharing what you know. Talk about your sumo's competition. Talk about where the company's market is headed, changes that are coming, and how the competition is reacting, as a way to demonstrate your knowledge and to give some value for listening to you, so that this person will keep listening. Knowing what is going on in the company's market is definitely something on this person's plate, so by offering useful facts and figures, you're avoiding a no again. Keep him or her on the call as long as possible, so that the discussion becomes more information sharing than a lecture. Find out whether you can get an in-person meeting or whether there is another hoop to jump through first.

Providing something of value up front, such as information about the company's market or competition, is the way of the BD professional. The goal is to get some useful intelligence about the company's operations or decision-making process in exchange. While there's no guarantee that anything useful will transpire, BD professionals always give something of value first. It's an indirect way to get to a discussion and build a relationship for a potential alliance.

On the other hand, talking immediately about what you have to sell is how salespeople lead off the call. There's little lead-in or preliminary exchange. They can be more direct in their approach because they have something tangible that they know the person on the other end of the line needs or buys. So they cut to the chase: "Do you want paper cups or not?" If not, they move on to the next name on the prospect list to call. Sales is a numbers game. For example, you may make 100 calls to get, on average, say, 40 proposals, worth about $500 of paper cups and a closing probability of 40 percent. It's dialing for dollars, because there are hundreds or thousands of sales prospects who are a good fit for what you have to offer.

BD is different because there are so few companies or potential partners that can actually do what you need them to do or that have the resources critical for your project to be a success. Take the recent Salesforce.com and Twitter alliance, for example. Salesforce has a social intelligence application that can monitor in real time what people are saying about companies and their products or services on social media websites, such as Twitter, Facebook, LinkedIn, and YouTube, and on blogs and in web forums. Salesforce compiles data based on what's being disseminated on these sites, so an alliance with one of their major data sources—Twitter—makes perfect sense. Alliances with Facebook, LinkedIn, and other consumer opinion sites, such as Yelp or epinions, would also make sense. Alliances with sites such as Yamaha or Kelly Services or Burberry, which are Salesforce.com customers, would not; there is little or no overlap in core competency or market. There are probably only a handful of companies that are a smart fit for what Salesforce currently does. It's not a numbers game.

Finding a good match, a good alliance partner, takes knowledge and digging, and it can take time. But you're not in a rush. You want to be sure a partnership makes sense for both your company and your partner company. So you may have several phone conversations spanning a number of months as you try to get to know your key contact and develop a relationship. During that time, you also want to ask for a face-to-face meeting. It's much better to be in a room than to be on the phone. And you want it to be in that person's offices, not yours, in part to maintain control. If you invite your potential partner to come visit your offices, it may take a month or two before he or she can fit such travel into his or her schedule. But if he or she agrees to a meeting, you can and should make it a priority to be on a plane and at his or her doorstep in a matter of hours or days. My very supportive wife once asked me why I am always the one traveling to the prospective partners, versus asking them to come to me. My answer was simple, "Because I want them to be on my time line, and if I wait for them to come to me, then I am on their time line. If you can drop everything to go there, you can keep the process moving forward, rather than having it wither as your target's other priorities come up."

During the first meeting, you probably won't be in a conference room or big meeting space. It will more likely be in someone's office with a couple of people. You're still feeling each other out and building a case for your proposal. So you may or may not have a deck. This first meeting is really just a lead-in to the next meeting, the important meeting, where you'll work to secure several internal champions. During the initial meeting, you're trying to determine what the obstacles are to getting a yes. What will it take to get a yes? What do you need to share in order to move the needle forward? As much as you're an evangelist for your vision during this meeting, you're also taking a reading of where your contact is in his or her evaluation of the idea and what you still need to do to get another meeting.

But don't think getting that next meeting will be quick and easy. Far from it. A lot happens between your first introductions and the follow-up visit. Your contact will have internal discussions, you will have strategy discussions, he or she will e-mail you for clarification, and you will stay in touch by sending along relevant news. You will tease him or her with just enough detail to pique an interest—to bring up more questions—but not enough to lead to a no. This conversation often goes on for months before you get approval for another meeting. During this time, your contact is deciding whether he or she even wants to pursue this partnership. It's not a sure thing, and you'll need to stay top of mind if you want to have any chance of getting that second meeting.

Once you get approval for a next meeting, you'll want to go in prepared, presentation deck ready but never in hand. I never go in with printed presentations as handouts. Conversely, our head of sales at TrueCar *always* goes in with printed information. He is trying to get to a yes, and providing as much information as possible helps him get there. It's a different process. I want every eye looking at me at the front of the room, not jumping ahead, which is what always happens when people have a printout in front of them. This is your opportunity to build a business case for your proposal. You need to give the company's representatives enough information to get excited about the possibilities your project holds, without them getting mired in the details. You also don't want to give them enough information to say no. You'll want to withhold information for that reason. It all goes back to control. You need to control what and how much is said during this meeting so that you can get another meeting.

The reason to hold back on details in your proposal is to encourage questions. Questions that come up give you a window into what your prospects' pain point is, where they're thinking this may lead, and where they're skeptical. You want questions, so don't try to anticipate and answer all of them in your presentation. Hearing questions helps you understand what your audience's concerns are, which you can then build your next presentation around. That information is like a building block—the more you have, the stronger your presentation deck will be for the next meeting. Questions also give you the opportunity to repeat your points over and over again as part of your response. Watch how participants in your meeting react to your responses. Do you need to phrase your solution in a new way? Hit hard on one aspect of the proposal? Emphasize another?

Take notes after your meeting so that you'll be even better prepared for the next one, but don't expect it to come immediately. Your contact may not be inclined to give you that next meeting right away. Yes, you may have been asked to follow up to schedule the next meeting, but that doesn't mean he or she wants you back tomorrow. You may have a sense of urgency, but it's unlikely that he or she feels similarly. So when you call to follow up and inquire about that next meeting, start by asking probing questions: "Tell me what the others think," or "Sue mentioned something in the meeting that I did a little research on," and then share some new information. Or if you're following up by e-mail, bring up some intriguing new development or piece of information you uncovered that is definitely relevant to your discussions, and invite a call back. If you've left your contact wondering what the heck that new piece of information is, your odds of getting that call, and that next meeting, increase substantially. Humans are curious by nature, so certainly leverage that all you can, without being unprofessional. You want to keep providing reasons for your contact to get on the phone, to call you instead of e-mailing, or putting off getting in touch. Deals can take years to solidify, and the more contact you have, the sooner you'll get results and the better those results will be.

It took me four years to finalize a deal with *Consumer Reports*. We met three times over a three-year period. We would have a meeting, and every call I made afterward to follow up would not be returned. Ever. No one would ever call me back. Sure, I was irritated, but I kept at it. I sent e-mail after e-mail and made call after call in the hopes of keeping the project alive—but never really knowing what was going on inside the company. Finally, something happened internally that brought this project back to the fore, and I got a call back for another meeting. I actually had three more meetings before the big one that sealed the deal.

NEVER GIVE UP THE DECK

At the end of a meeting, when you've presented your deck and made your case, someone at the company may ask for a copy of your presentation. In fact, someone always asks for it. Under *no* circumstances should you leave your deck behind or allow copies to be made. This may sound counterintuitive, since you just spent hours prepping for the presentation, but do not ever leave your deck behind. Doing so hands over control of your information.

If you leave behind your presentation, you have just empowered someone else to present your vision. Do you think anyone can talk about your company and this opportunity better than you? Of course not. Whoever has possession can shape the information to make the case for or against your project or possibly to make no case at all. You don't yet understand the political dynamics within the company you are pitching. Perhaps your champion has no political clout whatsoever. Perhaps he or she has some but not enough to deal with objections by people with more. Once the presentation is out of your hands, you've lost control of the information exchange and the process as a whole.

That's not to say you shouldn't be willing to answer follow-up questions or be available at a moment's notice to address issues that arise, but you want to do that in person, not allow someone internally to be your representative. So when someone asks for a copy of the deck, explain that you can't leave it behind but that you'd be glad to come back in for another meeting whenever needed. "Just let me know when you need me and I'll be here" should be your response.

Granted, you're going to get a lot of surprised looks. Who says no to a request for a copy of a presentation deck? You do. And you protect yourself from getting a no based on information someone else provides. Because when you turn over a presentation deck, you're essentially turning over control regarding how your pitch is presented.

When you allow your deck to be shared, you're now relying on the person who has possession to accurately portray your vision. As this person is describing the potential of your idea, he or she may unwittingly weave in incorrect assumptions or information. But, for sure, he or she cannot go to bat for the idea the way that you can. You can't focus on not getting a no if you're not in the room, and it will eventually boil down to a decision when you're not in the room.

The fact is nothing really happens in the meeting. It's when you're not there, after the meeting, that the real discussion starts. That's when the dissenters, the naysayers, speak up. They may not voice their concerns during the meeting, but they certainly won't hold back once you're gone. And the problem is that sometimes negative personalities can attract others to their position; they can persuade people who were on your side to switch sides. So the last thing you want is to give those naysayers any power. The way to do that, to reduce their influence, is to arm your potential champions with enough information to tell the naysayers that they are misinformed or to clarify the key points you were trying to make. Best case, they can shut the troublemakers down. And if not, suggest that the fallback is to schedule another meeting to rehash the points of contention and to get things straightened out. The key is to get the issues addressed and then get them resolved.

SEALING THE DEAL ON YOUR TERMS

To keep the BD process moving forward toward an official deal, you've needed to maintain control. You've controlled information, the pace of progress, and access to you, and now as you near the end of the pitching process, you can't let up on control. As you start to finalize the terms of your deal, you need to insist on drafting a term sheet. Some organizations want to go straight to an agreement, a contract, and you need to resist this at all costs. You have to create a term sheet first. It's critical.

The first reason to start with a term sheet is to maintain control of the process, but, more importantly, it's a way for you and your proposed partner to be sure you see eye to eye on key issues before the attorneys get involved in drafting anything and adding legalese. Term sheets spell out, in plain English, what each side is agreeing to—the terms of your agreement. However, a term sheet is not contractually binding. It's an intermediate step to confirm that everyone is clear about each partner's responsibilities. Once it is created, it is then used as the basis for an agreement or contract.

Throughout the pitch process, constantly be asking yourself, "By doing this, will I lose control, maintain control, or gain control?" Then act accordingly to try to always maintain or gain control and never lose it. Losing control means that someone else has taken the lead in determining whether your project is a go or not. You never want that decision, or that control, in anyone else's hands. Keep it in yours as long as possible.

5

COURTING THE SUMO

How do you get a market leader, a multinational company, to take your BD pitch seriously when they've never heard of you? That's the situation TrueCar faced in 2006 with Amazon. We were a start-up with a business proposal that could give any company unique entrée into the automotive market. Amazon was potentially our big sumo, but they were unsure that aligning with an early stage venture was a smart idea. No matter how relevant our pitch, the folks at Amazon weren't going to partner with a pure start-up, they told us. End of story.

So TrueCar began brainstorming how to get past this major objection. There was no way we could change the fact that we were a start-up—that was the reality of our situation—and Amazon execs, rightfully so, perceived the risk of failure to be too great when dealing with a new business. Their objection made sense, and it also opened a door for us, perhaps unbeknownst to Amazon. By telling us that our start-up status was the roadblock, they led us to a work-around, which was to find an established and respected business partner to work with us in pursuing Amazon. If we didn't have enough credibility ourselves to get a foot in the door, we'd borrow it from a known entity.

So we turned to AutoTrader, one of the leaders in online automotive, and proposed that they partner with us on a response to Amazon. While letting Amazon know that we were bringing in an as-yet unnamed substantial partner, we negotiated with AutoTrader to bolster our position with Amazon. When we returned to Amazon, together, to explain how Amazon could be different, how they could leapfrog the competition with our approach, this time they took us seriously. We weren't an unproven start-up; we were the creative force behind a collaboration with an automotive powerhouse, AutoTrader.

The situation is a lot like courting in the Victorian era, where a gentleman had to request permission to date a lady he was interested in. The odds of a young man receiving permission if he was new to the town—a virtual unknown—were nil. What parents would allow their child to spend time with someone they didn't know? Very few. Yet, if that same gentleman turned to his uncle, the town mayor, for help in gaining permission, perhaps through a personal endorsement, the parents would be much more likely to be welcoming of a courtship proposal. It's often not what you know but whom you know. And if you're trying to get close to a sumo, you may want someone else with credibility to back you up.

Partnering first with a well-known organization to pursue a mutual client is one way to gain instant credibility for your own company. By formally associating your company with a more prominent organization, you're borrowing the reputation and authority to improve your odds of growing your business or, in our case, landing more BD deals. That's the reality. You need the other organization to help you reduce the perceived risk potential that partners see when considering your pitch. It all comes down to positioning, really, and the enhanced stature it immediately earns you.

Working to identify and partner with a better-known ally in an effort to pursue and land a mutual client is what I call "triangular attraction."

TRIANGULAR ATTRACTION AS A STRATEGY

If your business is too new or too unknown to capture the attention of a desirable BD partner, you could invest time and energy in boosting your visibility, such as via a major PR campaign, advertising blitz, or pricey sponsorship. Or you could take a shortcut and simply tap into the credibility another organization has already earned. This is really the essence of BD—cooperating with another business to pursue a market or opportunity that neither of you is currently serving.

So if you're struggling to get an initial meeting with your contact at a target BD prospect, consider, instead, identifying larger, complementary companies that have expertise that could be valuable to your project. I call these alliance partners, and they are not always the biggest and most obvious choice. You are looking for a capability that carries credibility.

Need a search engine powerhouse? Google may not need anyone, but those competing with Google might be interested in your ideas and a way to capture new customers. Want to be able to tap into the market for professional photographers? Nikon or Canon may be obvious companies to start with, but what about the company that manages Santa Claus photos at malls during Christmastime? There are always options. Your alliance partners don't need to play a major role, but you need to be able to position them as collaborators in your BD venture.

While most potential BD partners will initially say no to your requests for meetings, you'll have much more success in approaching an alliance partner. The reason is that they have less to lose. You've lined up the BD partner, have had conversations, have outlined a proposed project, and simply need your collaborator to fill a void and help you finalize an agreement. You've done the heavy lifting, and now they just need to help seal the deal. Of course, it's rarely that easy. But you're handing over a potentially large opportunity to a collaborator, and most will at least consider working with you. However, the process of approaching them, pitching them on pursuing your BD target, and outlining your respective roles still needs to occur.

Once you've found your alliance partner and formalized your collaboration, start name-dropping to your potential partner. During your follow-up phone calls, or as part of e-mail messages, mention that Big Name Collaborator has now agreed to partner with you on your proposed project. Highlight some of your collaborator's claims to fame or core expertise that will be instrumental in making your joint project a success. Confirm that this collaboration is exactly why the BD deal is going to be successful, and then ask for the meeting. Then ask for another meeting.

NEGOTIATING FOR CREDIBILITY

In cases where you're having difficulty landing a collaborator, it may be in your best interest to pit two or more companies against each other—in a competition for a partner role. Rather than doggedly pursuing one collaborator at a time, pursue each simultaneously, and don't keep it a secret. As in courting, fuel some friendly competition by letting other suitors know what you're looking for in a mate. Let the other(s) know that you're looking for a collaborator that can do X, Y, and Z and you'll be choosing the company that will give you the best chances of success in consummating a BD deal with a mutual partner. Be clear that you're going to choose one or the other and that the preferred partner will reap a number of rewards, not the least of which is a shot at landing a major BD partner as their partner as well. That way, you can play one against the other, making the opportunity to collaborate with your company that much more desirable to both companies.

Here is how the process of landing a sumo by using triangular attraction might work.

Let's say your company is a start-up with the goal of solving computer virus problems for consumers and small businesses. You provide service and support in addition to software. In order to launch your company, you need to partner with an antivirus (AV) software company *and* a warranty company to handle the insurance and claims administration. Both of your target companies are billion-dollar businesses, and you have raised $250,000 of angel funding.

The players: Sumo A is a prominent antivirus software company. Sumo B is a prominent warranty company.

This is how your first phone pitch might go:

> **You**: Thanks for taking my call. I'm developing a new solution to address computer viruses that goes beyond software. Of course, I want to include software in my solution, and I want to talk to you about partnering to include your award-winning AV software as part of my value proposition.
>
> **Sumo A**: What type of solution are you talking about? How do you go "beyond" just a software solution?
>
> **You**: The software is nice, but consumers are most worried about fixing the problem. And, as you know, the software can prevent only what it has already identified, and if the consumer does not update the software regularly, the computer is virtually defenseless. We are building out an insurance solution—think of it as a warranty. We promise our customers, "If a virus damages your computer, we'll fix it for free!" Rather than focus on software, we provide free tech support and free local repair at more than 8,000 locations nationwide.
>
> **Sumo A**: How do you have 8,000 locations?
>
> **You**: The other company we are working with is Sumo B. They are one of the largest consumer electronics warranty providers in the country. They currently provide warranties for X, Y, and Z. They process more than five million claims a year. We will leverage their

call center, claims systems, underwriting, and, of course, computer repair network.

Sumo A: We sell our software in those retail locations now. Why would we want to support a competing product?

You: There are many AV software companies. You are the largest because of your brand recognition. The consumers know nothing of how your software works. But they recognize you and therefore trust your software over all the others. In our case, the software brand is irrelevant. Consumers are choosing the product based on the value proposition: "If you get hit with a virus, we will fix it for free!" At that point, we could include any software. The choice is no longer about the trust in the software; it's about the trust in the guarantee behind it.

Sumo A: I'm not sure we want to be involved in this.

You: I understand. You need to make the right decision for your company, but I can tell you that with Sumo B behind this, our product will launch and will be in all of these retail outlets. They are serious about the warranty business, and this represents an opportunity for them to get into solving the "soft" issues, versus just warranting the hardware purchase. This is a huge opportunity for us, for them, and, I believe, for you, too. That's why we are talking. This is going to happen whether you are part of it or not. Why don't we at least schedule a meeting where I can come in and explain it to you and your team in more detail?

You can also convey the fact that you're evaluating other potential partners and can assure your target sumo that whichever company you choose, they will be a well-known leader with core competencies key to the success of your BD project. At each step of the evaluation, you can also take the opportunity to inform your BD target of your progress as a way to stay top of mind. Once you narrow your choices to two or three companies, let each of them know. If you've negotiated some deal terms that will save your BD target money or help some part of their business, make sure you tell them that.

In addition to making you a more attractive BD partner, borrowing credibility from more established companies also makes you a more powerful competitor. Using BD, you can dominate your market, make your competitors almost inconsequential, and make future BD deals that much easier to secure.

GOING IT ALONE

Triangular attraction is not a method you will use very often, as it does not always apply. But courting your sumo does involve building a story that helps reduce the perceived and actual risk to the sumo. Triangular attraction is one way to reduce that perceived risk, demonstrating momentum in a specific category. Although there is always risk involved in any business deal, if there is too much perceived risk, you'll get a quick no. Focusing on the huge payoff when success is achieved is one strategy to keep sumos interested; they're all about winning.

Another approach is to replace one of the collaborators with your value proposition. Your BD target may aspire to connect with the capabilities of a large player in its space, but you may not be able to get that company to join as an alliance partner. Still, you believe that your opportunity could bring the same results. Present your opportunity as if your vision is as attractive as the biggest and most powerful sumo in the industry. That is, you are offering an opportunity as good as partnering with Google and Apple. It's that important to their future growth, and there is no way the partner should consider saying no without sitting through a full presentation.

COURTING CAUTIONS

When you're courting a sumo, there are a variety of things you need to remember. First, as an early stage entrepreneur, you and your company have limited resources. These courtships can take a long time to result in a pairing, and, unlike with sales, I never recommend filling a large queue of prospects until your company is in the mode to scale its BD initiative. You simply don't have the resources to be pursuing many sumos simultaneously.

Caution #1: Don't Fill Your Queue

There are generally two or three companies deserving of your time and attention and that make strategic sense for you to pursue. Go after them and be confident that you will close a deal with at least one. To pitch, you need conviction, a complete belief that this will happen. When you know you've found "the one," don't stop pursuing it until a deal is sealed. Going after too many at one time makes it easier to walk away from the one you really want. To quote Napoleon Hill, "No one is ever defeated until defeat has been accepted as a reality."

Caution #2: Don't Chase Revenue

Second, too many entrepreneurs start chasing revenue too soon. You may think that the sumo with the largest potential revenue is the obvious one to pursue first. Not so fast. Consider the strategic impact before the revenue. Why? Because the revenue does not materialize overnight, unless, of course, you are in one of these unique situations where the sumo wants to guarantee you revenue to lock you up from their competition. So short of that, you'll get more "play" out of your limited efforts by assessing and then leveraging the strategic impact of the partnership.

CAUTION #3: DON'T TAKE PARTNERS THAT DON'T BUILD MOMENTUM

In the early stages, entrepreneurs have a tendency to chase deals, any deals. Why? Because we want deals! But, there's a downside to this. As I said, use BD to eventually get the market to converge on you. This means that your targets "feel" your presence and your deal flow and believe that they need to work with you. That message gets diluted when you've partnered with meaningless companies in too many verticals. Don't water down your market presence. Focus on "owning" a market or category. And if you are in the process of raising money, you have to show traction with the limited resources you have in place. You will sound so much more powerful if you can claim that you signed three sumos in the cellular retail category versus a three-sumo portfolio made up of one cellular retail group, one pool supply retail group, and one dry cleaning retail group. The former shows a coordinated BD strategy, while the latter could be perceived as luck.

BE SELECTIVE

When you're courting, you are assessing the fit between your company and the sumo. You're determining whether a partnership makes sense, given the resource commitment it will take to be successful.

The sumo, on the other hand, is thinking more about minimizing the downside risk than about the upside potential. While a pairing can double or triple your company's valuation, it's unlikely to have as transformative an effect on a sumo that is already an industry leader; from the sumo's perspective, the downside risk is much larger. So in this courting phase, one of your challenges is reducing their perceived risk. You want to keep the conversation going, continue to schedule meetings, and stay as far as possible away from a no. Take baby steps toward a relationship. Because while you want to keep pushing the relationship forward, it is very easy for sumos to say no and shut down future conversations. Don't let that happen.

6

CREATING CONFUSION

Marketing communications experts extol the virtues of clarity in business. The clearer you are about your message, your product or service's benefits, its potential applications, and your target market, the more successful you will be, they tell us. While this may be true in a sales environment, in fact, the opposite is true in BD. In BD, the right amount of ambiguity can be your greatest strength.

Strategic ambiguity is your goal during the BD pitch process and throughout most of the negotiation phase. As you're presenting your vision for a partnership with the sumo in front of you, the last thing you want to do is to be overly specific about what you are proposing. Sounds counterintuitive, doesn't it? In this case, the reason is that being overly specific in the early stages of a discussion makes it easier for someone to say no. The more your prospective partner company thinks they understand how you will achieve all the results you are promising, the more likely they are to introduce their preconceived, often inaccurate notion of why it won't work. This may be because they doubt you can do it, because they don't like your work process, because they think they can do it better themselves, or maybe simply because they didn't like the Gantt chart you used on your presentation slides. So don't get so specific. Clarity can bite you in the ass.

Confusion, however, holds everyone's attention. As your audience struggles to comprehend your proposal, they are engrossed in what you are saying. They're listening for details that will aid them in grasping the big picture. That's what you want. You are telling a story and leading them down a path. Your path.

By holding back information, rather than handing it to partners on a silver platter, you keep them engaged. You keep the dialogue flowing, the questions and answers, the "what ifs," and the brainstorming. You provide the big picture—the 35,000-foot view of the partnership—rather than the granular detail. It's much harder to dispute or disagree with talk of possibilities or potential, but specifics can quickly be ripped apart.

Few sumos will balk at a vision of accelerated growth and market leadership, while nearly everyone will want to give his or her two cents about how that will come to pass. So don't get into those discussions right now. Keep the information high level and vague. At this stage, ambiguity and imprecision are your friends.

By keeping the project specifics vague, you also maintain control. When you are the only person in the room who has a clear picture of what a partnership would look like and how it will benefit all involved, you have power. You are the expert. No one else in the room knows as much as you do about your vision, and that is exactly how you want it. No one else can pitch your vision better than you can, so you want to prevent someone else from turning around and speaking for you to management, thinking that he or she knows what you know. Make it clear that no one else does. The best way to do that is to hold back on details. Keep the fire burning—keep the discussion moving forward—and give oxygen when it is needed but only in measured doses.

The truth is control and confusion are two sides of the same coin. Your goal is to keep your sumo confused in order to maintain control of the information flow and the BD process. When you know more than everyone else in the room, you are the leader. Others almost *have* to listen to you. Control and confusion have the same aim but are two different approaches that are the most effective when used together.

Interestingly, actual sumo *rishiki* (sumo wrestlers) in Japan use a variation of this technique. When you watch a sumo wrestling match, it appears that the sumos are massive weight powered by pure brute strength, but that's not really the case. They train diligently to be able to keep their hands, arms, and shoulders relaxed so they don't alert their opponent to which way they are going to move next. They can keep their opponent in the dark until they are ready to make their move. They can then get the upper hand with the other wrestler by not warning him in advance about their strategy. It's a variation of the confusion tactic applied in the ring. The sumo is a lot more strategic than he appears at first glance.

FOCUS ON THE SUMO'S MISSION

Several years ago, a major Internet sumo brought in a new management team to turn the company around. We at TrueCar approached a new senior executive at the company about partnering, picturing a deal where TrueCar's platform could power the site's auto-buying program. As I pitched it, I kept emphasizing the executive's mission—bringing about change throughout the company. He wanted specifics to bring to his CEO and was nervous about signing off on a radical deal so early in his tenure. So I asked, "Are you trying to make your company relevant or continue to have it be irrelevant?"

That question creates confusion. Of course, he wants the company to be relevant. Who wouldn't say that?! He still had no idea how a partnership with my company would be the best course of action to achieve that goal, but I now owned the idea of that in his mind. If he wanted his company to be relevant, he would need to work with us to achieve that, his subconscious would remind him. It's very unlikely that any other company we were competing with for this partnership positioned the relationship quite that way. They most likely employed a sales approach, including citing metrics on visitors, how much money is generated, etc. We were the only ones offering to look at the bigger picture, with a vision for how to make this sumo better. That's the real beauty of BD.

REELING YOUR TARGET IN

At each step of the decision-making process, your BD target may decide they need to do more research. That's fine, but you want to remain involved in that process, too. Remind them that, because of the confusion, you may say, "If a question comes up, feel free to call or e-mail me." Because of the confusion, you know this will happen. You want to remain involved in the process. That's where confusion helps. You already know the questions will come up because you've set it up that way.

They're going to need to call you—that's a given. You want them to ask you to come back in to explain something. Questions will come up, and you want to be involved in the process so that you can personally resolve any open questions or issues in your way, with your words, your vision. You're starting to hear more concerns and objections, and you're able to solve them as they're happening.

This process is a lot like reeling in a big fish. You want to attract its attention with some bait—something really attractive. Once it decides to take a nibble, you start trying to get it on the line without it breaking; when the line breaks, you've gotten a no. Keeping the line intact takes sharing bits and pieces of details about your deal's potential or, in fishing terms, chumming, to draw the fish near. Then let up a little to give your target time to go away and assess what it would mean for them. Then you check in and drop another detail that piques their interest, all the while driving them toward the boat, where you'll catch them in a net.

What you *don't* want to do is put some tasty bait on the line and then start reeling them in as fast as you can, before they've even come close enough to sink the hook. That's a sales approach, not BD. Partners need enough information about the proposed project to be interested, but overwhelm them and they'll start swimming in the opposite direction. Then you're left with nothing, and the fish in the water is still hungry, still open to tasting bait dangled by other anglers.

What could be worse than a sumo walking away from your deal? That same sumo deciding to partner with your largest competitor.

The last thing you want to do is to hand over a very specific project game plan early on that your sumo can then shop around to the competition. Keep the information level vague until you have the fish on the line, virtually swimming toward the waiting boat as you lead it along.

LEVERAGING CONFUSION

The frequency of communication during a BD deal negotiation ebbs and flows. If you're communicating with your sumo regularly, the information you share is in the form of sound bites that they can easily repeat internally to keep the project moving forward. If the frequency of communication has slowed, however, your focus needs to shift to intriguing them again—getting them back on the line. The type of information you share is different when you're working in parallel to seal a deal than when you're trying to reengage a partner.

For example, you might tell your BD target, "You can be the market leader if you work with us." If they've been an also ran for many years, becoming the market leader may sound pretty attractive. "What do you mean we can be the market leader?" they ask you. And you reply, "Let's get together and I'll lay it all out for you." Then when you meet, you restate that they can be the market leader and share a few nuggets but hold back on much of the specifics. You give enough new information to increase their interest without enough to have them walk away. Then you try to get a second meeting, telling them you want to share the specifics with their management team. Keep it vague, dropping facts here and there to demonstrate that you know the industry but without getting into how, exactly, you can help them become the market leader.

If your BD partner begins to question whether you really can make such promises, instead of providing specifics about how you'll accomplish what you've discussed, tell stories about what you've achieved in the past to build credibility. "How are you so confident you can get this done?" they may ask. And instead of laying out the step-by-step plan you may have for them, you tell them about past successes. "Well, we've raised millions of dollars from these promi-nent venture capitalists (borrowing credibility), I have this sumo aligned with us (triangular attraction), our management team is made up of serial entrepreneurs who have worked in this space for 15 years, and we don't fail (evangelic conviction), so I'm extremely confident in what I'm telling you," you can say. And then introduce some doubt about their interest in the deal. "You can miss the win-dow or not, but this will happen. We're well funded. We've got the right investors, the track record, and the partners, and we will do this. The question is whether you want to be part of it. We have other interested partners that we will go to, but we are talking with you now because you are the right one for this opportunity." That kind of push back and questioning can reengage them.

Of course, if you get questions about your own company, specifics are fine. There's no need to be vague or confusing about what you've done and whom you've worked with, as long as it is to your benefit. Choose to position your situation in the best possible light. Don't say you've raised a little bit of funding. Say you have angel backers and name-drop when possible. Don't say you've raised $2 million when, instead, you can say you've "received a multimillion-dollar investment from a fund with deep pockets that is prepared with a follow-on investment after we hit the next milestone." Remember that, during this phase, people look for reasons to say no and move on. You're still being honest and specific, but you're spinning it to demonstrate your momentum and dedication to the vision.

CONTROL IS THE CONCEPT, CONFUSION THE TACTIC

Confusion is king when you're talking about the particular deal on the table, about the "how." A partner might say to you, "Tell me more about how this technology works." And depending on where you are in the negotiation, you may not want to share much. So you could say, "I'm not going to share with you how the technology works yet, but what I can share with you is how the program would work for your customers, why they need this, the demand we anticipate, and anything else about the program you might want to know." Then, to demonstrate you're open to getting more specific in the future, you could say, "Now, if you want to move forward on having deeper discussions, let's sign a nondisclosure agreement."

That said, I think nondisclosures are, from a legal perspective, a waste of paper, so don't spend a lot of time modifying language in this document. They are hard to hold up in court, unless you can prove that your partner disclosed confidential information out in the public. That's hard to do. What I think nondisclosures are good for is to establish a hurdle for your partner to get past. It's one more milestone, one step toward commitment, one more yes.

KEEPING THE PROCUREMENT DEPARTMENT AT ARM'S LENGTH

As you and your BD partner get closer to reaching agreement, many companies will bring in their procurement department to manage the final sign-off. While procurement professionals are experts at managing sales transactions, they are out of their element when it comes to BD partnerships. Know that going in. They are not experts in your area, whether it's software development, real estate, e-commerce, or any other field. What they are experts in is *their company's process* for procuring products and services from vendors.

Although you are the expert here, suddenly procurement is in charge of your deal. They will try to dictate terms, veto key elements of your agreement, and generally try to convert your agreement between two peers into a typical vendor-client contract. You are not a vendor, and you should not sign a contract that suggests that you are. You are not subservient to your BD partner, no matter how much easier that would make the procurement department's job.

Also, keep in mind that procurement cannot say no to you. Generally, they do not have the power. So they cannot kill your agreement even if they wanted to because they are a support resource. They are there to hammer out the details of an agreement a particular business unit desires. They can delay the finalization of the deal by inserting unnecessary terms and conditions that you do not want there, but they can't refuse to negotiate with you. Here is where confusion saves the day.

Instead of trying to make changes to the contract directly, explain why their language does not apply and provide the language their own business unit wants to see. Blame the change on their own employees—your future partners. By pushing back and offering alternate language, you can try to force procurement to schedule a meeting with the business unit and you. If you confuse them with your terminology, you can try to regain control of where the agreement is going.

WINNING RFPS

Confusion can also be useful when responding to a request for proposal (RFP). You don't ever want to try to land a BD partner through an RFP, because you are not a vendor and you do not want to be perceived in that role. Nor do you want to be responsive or reactive to their request, rather than leading the process. But you *can* use an RFP as a springboard to get a conversation started.

An RFP can be useful for alerting you to situations where your idea, your partnering opportunity, may be a fit. But you do not want to respond to an RFP the way everyone else on the list is responding. No, you want to use the opportunity to present your completely new and different view of their organization as it will look once you two are partnered. So instead of diligently responding to each of the questions in the RFP, take the opportunity to explain your alternate solution. Don't go into too much detail, so as to give them a reason to reject your idea outright, but suggest a completely different approach than what they had originally pictured. Answer the questions you wish they had asked, rather than what's on the paper, and offer enough information so that they can start to envision what your solution looks like. The RFP is a chance to turn the questions around and highlight value propositions that no one else can replicate. Your goal is to intrigue them. You're not trying to win the bid; your goal is to get them to throw out the RFP and start talking to you instead.

Let's say, for example, a sumo issues an RFP in search of a technology solution that will improve their online retail experience. Now, you may have nothing to do with technology that enhances a consumer's online shopping experience, but if you have something related that achieves the same end, you can use the RFP to at least get your proposal read.

Where a salesperson would respond line by line to each RFP question, you're going to answer the questions but introduce a new vision for the solution. You're going to describe how your solution could work, why it provides the best possible online shopping experience, and what it will take to make such a system a reality. You give them only the eagle's-eye view—the picture of "here's what's possible." Done well, that's all you need.

When you get a call from the contracting officer with questions about your response to the RFP, don't rush to answer. "It's complicated" is a much better answer or "No, you can't do that, but there are other approaches." It's OK if this creates confusion. Then you push for a meeting. "I'll be in town next week, so why don't we set something up and I can explain it more fully." If you get push back, don't back down. "I'm not going to give you details over the phone or put them in writing without having an understanding of where you want to go," you can explain. Or, you can say, "There is proprietary information I'm not willing to put into a document. I'm not interested in arming you with a lot of ideas about why everyone is headed in this direction, only to have you take that information and hand it to someone else." If you get resistance to a meeting, you can say something like, "If you're making the decision to pass this up because you're not willing to have a meeting to discuss a larger opportunity, then perhaps your company does not want to be the leader in its space—or have a competitive advantage—or maintain its leadership position, etc. Are you really going to ignore this opportunity because you don't want to have a half-hour meeting?" In most cases, they won't say no to a meeting, especially if you've piqued their interest enough.

In several cases, we've had RFPs thrown out after we submitted our proposal and then were asked for a meeting. By making the vision of what's possible so enticing, so appealing, that they couldn't say no, you can work around an existing RFP. But it starts with confusion, with not playing by the rules, and with sidestepping the required questions listed on the RFP. By the way, I have never lost an RFP in my entire career.

One of the first deals I did at TrueCar was with a powerhouse organization that serves the military and their families with superior financial and insurance products. I referred to them earlier as Big Sumo 1. Executives at Big Sumo 1 walk the walk. They care about their members (nine million and growing). Every product they launch must have a near 100 percent member satisfaction rating, or it gets reviewed and revised or sunsetted. By far, Big Sumo 1 is TrueCar's most important relationship; it has evolved to include a large investment and board representation. But it all started with an RFP asking for information on a piece of web technology.

TrueCar did not specialize in what Big Sumo 1 was after; we wanted to pursue a much broader solution—an auto-buying program that included a national network of Big Sumo 1-certified dealers. So my approach to their RFP was to respond with everything but what they were asking for in the RFP. The questions in the RFP became meaningless because I was thinking so much bigger for them. They were thinking about providing their members with information about features, options, and the manufacturers' suggested retail price (MSRP) of a vehicle. I was thinking about allowing their members to get a guaranteed up-front price on any car they were looking for, with full integration into their Big Sumo 1 loan information, and then to connect them with a certified dealer that would treat their members like gold, deliver the car at that price, and ensure that both Big Sumo 1 and the members get everything they needed. They asked for a web tool, and I offered something completely different in my RFP response.

Rather than being thrown out as nonresponsive, my proposal started a conversation with Big Sumo 1. Yes, in fact, responding to their RFP with different information than what was requested worked. There was much more for Big Sumo 1 to do, but we were now positioned as their perfect partner. And to throw some icing on the cake, TrueCar was the first non-AAA rated company to ever work with Big Sumo 1. We were a start-up and years away from profitability, and they were ranked as the number-one customer service brand in the country. That's how effective a BD effort can be.

Confusion can be extremely effective in BD. By keeping sumos confused, you maintain control. They don't know where you're coming from, where you're headed, and what you'll do next, which is what makes you hard to knock out of the ring. So instead, they consider partnering with you. If you're that attuned to what will make them even more effective competitors, they'd be fools not to.

7

TYING THE KNOT
WITH YOUR SUMO

Sometimes, even when both partners have outlined and agreed to all the terms of their relationship, problems can arise during the eleventh hour of a negotiation. You're actually never done negotiating with partners, even after the agreement is in place and you have started working together. But before a contract is signed, while you're defining what your collaboration will entail, the best way to deal with potential issues is to prepare a detailed term sheet.

THE IMPORTANCE OF THE TERM SHEET

Once you and your potential partner get to a point where you're asking, "What would a deal look like?" it's time to consider drafting a term sheet. In some cases, a partner will bring up a term sheet far too early in the process, when you really haven't fully explored all the project parameters. In that case, you want to put off developing a term sheet for a bit. Creating one prematurely can kill the deal by giving your partner the opportunity to say no to some of the proposed terms.

When you get to the term sheet, there should be little push back on items covered, because you've already discussed them. The term sheet itself is simply a written version of what you've been discussing. If you have been working toward a deal for more than a year and it seems a foregone conclusion that you will come to agreement, a term sheet is the next logical step. It is at this point that you stop avoiding the no and start focusing on getting a yes.

Some companies fast-forward to an official binding agreement and skip the term sheet altogether. Under no circumstances should you do this. The problem with skipping the term sheet is that you skip straight to a contract. That means that attorneys immediately get involved, which is the last thing you want.

When you start negotiating through redlines in a contract, you are headed for disaster. Negotiating point by point in a contract is a bad move because (1) it takes so much longer; (2) there is more friction because you're approaching the situation as adversaries, not partners; and (3) lawyers get involved, which you absolutely do not want. Sumo lawyers take control very quickly.

One of the major benefits of a term sheet is that lawyers need not be involved. The language used in a term sheet is conversational, not legalese. It can be as simple as an e-mail that lists all that you are agreeing to and all that your partner is agreeing to and a statement regarding what will happen as a result of the two companies working together. The moment it starts sounding like a binding contract, your partner will want to get lawyers involved and the process will slow to a halt. You don't want lawyers coming anywhere near your term sheet at this stage. They can get involved later, once you have everything ironed out and clear between you and your partner. But for now, keep it simple.

Term sheets can be one page, two pages, even three pages long if they must be, but the key is to keep the language conversational. The point of creating a term sheet is to iron out any questions or concerns either partner has about the relationship, the obligations to each other, what happens if things go really well, and what happens if they don't go so well. You want to address any points of contention now and get them resolved, in language everyone understands. So you'll cover what the revenue share is, how long the partnership will last, what the marketing obligations are to each other, what kind of exclusivity is promised, and any other service-level agreements that are required. There should be no mention of limits of liability and indemnification; those are for lawyers to address after all the business terms have been finalized.

When everyone agrees that the term sheet reflects the desired partnership, it's time to turn the process over to lawyers. At that point you generally use a shell agreement or template that the lawyers fill in. As the entrepreneur, your preference should be to use your template, rather than the sumo's, because many companies pull out their standard master services agreement as their starting point, which does not apply to your situation. Their vendor agreement is not what you want to sign. You're not a vendor; you're a partner, so much of that kind of agreement will need to be stricken or changed. However, if you start discussions using your template, fewer changes will likely be needed.

Another way to approach the situation is to offer to draft an agreement in the next week. Most sumos won't be able to crank out anything in fewer than three or four weeks, so some will leave it in your hands for the sake of speed. It also makes sense for you to draft it because you're the company that envisioned the project to begin with; you know more about the scope of the partnership, who is responsible for what, what needs to happen, and so on. These are all reasons why it makes more sense for you to take the first pass.

Unfortunately, in many cases, the sumo will insist—*Insist!*—that their legal team must draft the agreement. Of course, when this occurs, the lawyers will add all sorts of clauses obligating you to terms you would never agree to or restricting you from activities that would hamper your business. This is when the redlining begins—when you start tearing apart their contract draft.

To try to work around their insistence and still keep the process moving forward, suggest that you start with your shell but leave sections related to legal terms blank, for the sumo to add. Explain that this will help speed things up. Do all you can to maintain control of this part of the process. Yes, it will cost you more to hire a legal team to create a draft, but you won't be at the mercy of the sumo and their massive legal team. And if it is your responsibility to draft, you can also control how quickly the first draft gets back to your partner.

But sometimes even the term sheet can't overcome internal politics. Let me tell you a story about one such scenario.

THE IMPORTANCE OF ORGANIZATIONAL BUY-IN

TrueCar was trying to partner with a regional membership group (MG), which owned an auto-buying program they had been managing for several years. They had tried outsourcing before, and the service providers had not lived up to their obligations, so MG brought management responsibility back in-house. When we at TrueCar assessed the MG's program not long ago, we saw an opportunity to develop an even stronger auto-buying program that would blow their current product out of the water. So we pitched them. They listened. They were clearly intrigued but were also nervous about putting at risk the revenue the operation was currently generating, which was several hundred thousand dollars. So we agreed to guarantee their current level of profits. During the term of our agreement, they would never earn less than what they were currently earning.

We don't do this a lot, but in this case, we weren't talking about a lot of money in the relative scheme of things. We knew we would generate more than we were guaranteeing in the first year, and offering the guarantee was a way to overcome an objection and avoid getting a no on the deal. We were also confident in our business model, and we needed to help them get past any concerns they had about handing the program over to a third party again.

Of course, in addition to reducing your partner's risk of loss, guaranteeing a minimum revenue flow gives you the power to demand certain levels of performance on the partner's side, especially with respect to marketing. You can't guarantee revenue without assurances that the partner will provide sufficient marketing support to maintain at least their current level of performance. It's only reasonable, and that's how you present it. You may ask that they guarantee a certain level of web traffic or e-mail promotions, launch their website by a certain date, hit minimum quality levels, or follow other relevant marketing metrics. And you spell that out in the term sheet you'll draft, so that the obligations are crystal clear to everyone. There is no reason for you to eliminate their risk of loss while exposing yourself to loss because your partner decides they now don't have to do anything. It can happen.

Granted, they won't want to be contractually obligated to much; no one does. Still, you need to insist on it, or the deal as a whole will not make sense for you. Why would you put hundreds of thousands of dollars on the line without a promise from your partner that they will work equally hard to make the deal a success? You wouldn't. Stand firm in your demands. Be specific, too. Don't just demand that your partner give you "prominent" placement on their website. That is unclear. To you, prominence might mean on their home page, and to them, prominence might mean on page 15. Nail down the specifics so that there are no surprises later on that scuttle the deal entirely.

In the case of our MG deal, we negotiated back and forth for months. It took forever to get the details squared away, to sign the term sheet outlining exactly what everyone was agreeing to, and, then, when we all went to sign the final agreement, the CTO decided she did not want to be obligated to us. She wanted free reign over her technology domain and did not want to be beholden to us. At all. The business side of the company was ready to sign; they had no issues with the agreement. But the technology side of the company did not want to be hampered by us. They did not want a third party dictating what would be prominently featured on their company's website.

The conversation got heated at this point, which can happen in a BD deal. This is in stark contrast to a sales discussion, of course. In a sales conversation, a salesperson might ask, "What can we do to solve this challenge?" or "How do we get past this issue?" It is all about getting the sale. In a BD deal, however, the terms need to make sense for both sides. In this particular case, accepting the deal without any assurances from our partner that they would support us made no sense. I got pissed off. When I get pissed off, I tend to yell.

During this discussion, my goal was to talk some sense into my partners on the business side. I started by completely ignoring the CTO. She was no longer part of the conversation we were having as far as I was concerned. I told them:

> *"I'm surprised you're letting the technology side of your company—essentially an internal resource—make strategic business decisions about the future of your organization. Do they really have that power? Does tech run your company, or does business run your company?*

Because if tech is in charge, then you're not a partner we want to do business with.

"We have so many other partnerships we can do that we are not interested in partnering with a company that lets their resource side dictate their business strategy. You realize that she is blocking you from making $350,000 a year. You just lost $350,000. Are you willing to go to your CEO and tell him what you guys just did? Do you think he'll see that as a smart decision?

"MG has just become much less attractive to us as a partner, and I'm very comfortable walking away. Why don't you think about where your company is headed and whether you're serious about a partnership with us. If you are, call me back, but I'm not calling you."

We hung up.

Sure enough, the next day they called back and agreed to everything we had already outlined. Because it made sense. The CTO had attempted to block the negotiation because she was protecting her territory; it is a natural reaction when an outsider is encroaching on one of your responsibilities. No one likes it, including her, so she stepped in to try to prevent her freedom from being curtailed. But when I quantified the value of her decision to the company, which was $350,000, no one wanted to take the blame for turning down $350,000. And in this case, we were simply asking that the MG auto-buying program be as equally prominent on the MG home page as the most prominent MG product. We were not asking for TrueCar alone to be promoted, so this should have been an easy yes.

During negotiations you will undoubtedly encounter people who want to say no for the sake of saying no. They don't want to be obligated to anyone, even when such an obligation is beneficial to their company.

But when you are going to be financially obligated to pay them some amount of money, you want to be damn sure they are doing something in exchange to support that revenue. It doesn't make sense otherwise.

Now, let me make it clear that financial guarantees like the MG example are not the norm. Maybe 2–3 percent of my deals have involved a revenue guarantee and only when it was an easy "give" relative to the strategic and revenue upside. I want to merely point out that as you are negotiating a BD deal, you should look for ways to reduce your partner's concern about elements of the deal—in this case, the potential for lost revenue. That will increase your odds of being able to close the deal. But don't hand such obligations to them on a silver platter—ask for something in return to ensure they are equally committed and invested.

MARGINALIZING THE TROUBLEMAKER

When you are negotiating and you encounter people who want to have a say in the terms of the deal you are discussing when they really shouldn't, there are a number of techniques I use to cut them out. The first—simply ignoring them while I explain to my key contacts the danger of letting the troublemaker make decisions—works well. Another tactic, which I frequently use when lawyers try to change terms, is to question their role and call them out. You might say:

> *"I'm sorry, this is a business term. Why is the lawyer commenting now? I understand that your lawyer is here to protect you from a legal mistake, but this term has to do with whether we're going to do X, Y, or Z. It's not a legal issue. We've already agreed to it in the term sheet because you wanted A, B, and C. This isn't an indemnification clause or anything that legal needs to be involved in."*

Questioning why others get a say can be useful in retaining control of the process and helpful in supporting your negotiation counterpart. You want the businesspeople with the final say on non-legal issues as free as possible to finalize the deal you've been working on together.

I know I've spent some time here characterizing lawyers as difficult, so I must take a moment to clarify and praise the good ones. A lawyer's primary purpose is to protect his or her clients from risk. That's very important, and knowing that helps you to better understand your sumo's lawyers. Sumos have the most to lose. They have the reputation, the customers, the money, and the market share. You have close to nothing (relatively speaking), so there is a risk imbalance in the partnership. Large companies need to establish process and protocol. Therefore, their attorneys are accustomed to following the process and protocol.

In most cases, your partnership won't fit into a process or the defined protocol, and that's why you need to avoid their in-house counsel or procurement department until these unconventional terms are hammered out with your proposed partner.

As for your attorney, I assume you have a great one who understands that risk is important but that capitalizing on opportunity is the priority. Therefore, he or she knows that taking risk is part of your profile as an entrepreneur. We're talking not about risk that jeopardizes your business but about risk that enables growth. A good lawyer embraces the practical downside, not the nuclear downside, through strict interpretation of language. The sumo's attorney, on the other hand, leans toward strict interpretation, because the sumo has more to lose.

Your attorney is also there to make sure you don't get beaten up. He or she believes in the same philosophy related to a balanced multiyear strategic relationship and, as such, won't take shit from the bigger guy. Your attorney will call out the impractical and unreasonable nature of certain language in the same way that you have with your business counterpart. This may seem logical and sound obvious, but it's not. Also, don't assume that every attorney is equal. There are great ones and far too many acceptable ones. A great attorney makes the difference. Spend the money and find that great attorney.

AVOIDING BAD DEALS

Not all deals are good deals, however, and a deal that started out great can go sour little by little. They are the most dangerous, because BD deals are long-term arrangements. You invest time, money, and resources for an average of two to three years before you start generating serious revenue. Once that occurs, you may continue to partner for years after that. So from the start, you need to be sure that this is a company you want to work with and that the deal is one that will continue to be good for both parties for years to come.

In sales, you can take a penny-a-cup price cut on a single order for paper cups to help solidify your relationship with your customer, because you know you can make it back twice over on the next order. In the space of two or three years, you will likely have dozens of sales transactions with a satisfied customer, where you hopefully can correct any pricing imbalances. But it doesn't work that way on the BD side. You will have to live with the deal you are negotiating now for a long time. So being willing to take a significant reduction in your revenue, for example, when you receive nothing in exchange from your partner, can escalate into a major problem.

Sometimes you can try your best to avoid a deal you recognize as bad right away and you can still get pushed by senior management to make it. Maybe it's a top-down deal that you see from a mile away is going to be trouble. I've been there. Many years ago, one of my superiors wanted to do a deal with a major Internet player. They came to a rough agreement over 18 holes of golf one day and proceeded to insist that their teams formalize the details.

The key terms were that we were going to pay them $100 million over two years and they were, in turn, to provide key support for this initiative. The problem was that the only guys who thought this partnership was a good idea were the two senior execs. No one else on either side wanted to support it. It just didn't make sense for either company. Both sides tried to negotiate to make the deal fair, but it couldn't be done. Our partner was not interested in doing what was necessary to support it, nor, we discovered, were they technically capable. Three months into the partnership, the relationship fell apart. We wanted out, and they wanted their money. We spent a tremendous amount of "goodwill" equity to restructure the deal to be palatable. But the relationship was strained.

Unfortunately, the time and energy our team had to invest to make this deal good for us took our attention away from other company opportunities that could have been highly profitable. That is the major problem with bad deals—they eat away at your available resources. That's why it is better to walk away from an imbalanced deal than take it and hope for the best.

NEGOTIATING OUT THE TERMINATION FOR CONVENIENCE CLAUSE

One clause your partner will likely add is a cancellation for convenience clause. You may have several conditions under which your agreement will be considered null and void, such as for nonperformance of any kind or bankruptcy by either party. That is fairly typical. If you or your partner fails to live up to your terms of the agreement, all bets are off.

However, sumos like to keep their options open. They typically want to be able to cancel agreements because they feel like it. While this may be what they are used to, cancellation for convenience doesn't work for you. This is a long-term collaborative agreement, not a service contract, you need to explain. So you're not going to agree to invest your resources in a venture that does not have the complete support of both partners. That can't happen if one can back out at any moment. So cancellation for convenience is not an option. Ever.

Cancellation for cause, sure, that's fine. Or by mutual consent, yes. If things are not working out as anticipated and both partners agree to sever ties, that is fine. But allowing your partner to walk away without some kind of negative consequence would be damaging to your business.

Do you want to know the real reason why most sumos like to add a termination for convenience clause? Leverage! They want leverage over you down the road. As time goes on, they learn more about your business and the opportunity. Remember that you have the vision. You are the innovator. You are demonstrating future growth. If things go well and they are actually a factor in making your business grow, they may want to rethink the terms. Perhaps they should get 60 percent of the revenue generated through the partnership or, worse, start paying you a flat fee. You can't risk this. Lawyers and procurement departments don't think about the health of the relationship. They think about the words in a document—a document that the businesspeople should never need to revisit once it is signed. Do not ever agree to the convenience clause unless you are at full scale, where the incremental work is negligent and losing the partner midterm is irrelevant.

IF IT'S GOOD FOR YOU AND BAD FOR THEM, IT'S A BAD DEAL—PERIOD

Even deals that are clearly advantageous to you may not be deals you should pursue if, from the outset, your partner is at a disadvantage. Those are deals destined to fall apart in the future. Midway through the term of your deal, odds are good that your partner is going to recognize or perceive that they've been shafted and want out. So don't set yourself up for failure by trying to take a sumo to the cleaners. It won't end well.

Keep in mind that how you treat your partner during the negotiations sets the stage for the relationship going forward. To maintain a strong partnership, don't ask for terms you think are unreasonable. Stated another way, if you wouldn't agree to it, don't ask your partner to. Be fair.

Terms you would have a hard time convincing yourself to sign are what I call "bad-faith terms." They're hard to ask for because they don't usually make sense for one side. A prime example of a bad-faith term is the termination for convenience clause, which we just covered. Another example could be exclusivity, where the sumo wants to try to limit your growth for purely emotional reasons. Yet, at the same time, it could be very reasonable for you ask your sumo to be locked into your solution.

Most sumos, or large corporations, are not interested in being restricted but love the idea of restricting smaller companies for the sake of restricting them. They may claim that they want a unique advantage. They don't generally see the value of an exclusive agreement and typically don't have to agree to it when vendors or partners ask. And yet, my business won't do a deal unless it is exclusive, for a variety of reasons. One is our own value. Although we won't give exclusivity to others, we demand it from partners. Here is why.

When we agree to partner to power an organization's auto-buying program, we believe it is reasonable to ask that they not have more than one auto-buying program in place. Having multiple auto-buying programs would cannibalize the one that we manage, but that's not the primary reason why we insist on exclusivity. Our partners offering multiple solutions will result in massive confusion for their members. Given that we operate under the partner's brand as a white label and are held to strict service level agreements (SLAs), having multiple solutions puts us in the position to have to say to customers, "Sorry, but you did not use our service, so we can't help you." Additionally, imposing exclusivity on us would eliminate the benefits of group buying power and the network effect we can provide our partner. That is the argument for why we require exclusivity and yet don't agree to exclusivity ourselves.

All of these issues are brought up, discussed, and then captured in a term sheet that roughly outlines what the two partners may want to agree to. It is not set in stone, nor is it legally binding, but for the partnership to be a success, it is essential.

When you're done with the term sheet, then you head to the lawyers. You never relinquish control. Don't have your lawyer negotiate the rest of this. By your being on the phone, your business counterpart will also be on the phone. Don't just let lawyers handle it.

HOW TO DEAL WITH THE PROCUREMENT DEPARTMENT

In large companies, the department responsible for finalizing transactions, including business partnerships, is procurement. While procurement professionals are skilled at negotiating deals for paper cups and copy paper and laptops, they generally know very little about forging strategic partnerships. That's just not how they think. So when you bring them a draft agreement, they will try to insert themselves into the situation and take control. Of course, you need to maintain control of this deal or it will fall apart, so you can't let procurement take the helm.

The best way to do this is to confuse the shit out of them. You may have to work with them, but that doesn't mean you have to allow them to lead the way. To insert confusion, use language and terminology that they won't understand to describe the project, being as vague as possible. Your goal is to frustrate them so much that they have to turn back to their business owners (in their words, "the client") for clarification. You won't lose the deal because procurement can't understand the project. You'll only force them to reengage the businesspeople you've been dealing with. You want direct access to your business partners, which is what procurement will try desperately to prevent. But if you confuse them enough, they will have to turn it back over to the people you have been working with all along. Then, once your partners are back in the process, things can move ahead again.

In situations where procurement insists on terms that were never previously mentioned or that make no sense for your company, walk away. Explain to your contacts that "procurement killed the deal." "We agreed to the term sheet; we work with many other prestigious companies, such as X, Y, and Z, but apparently we're not qualified to do that for you, so we're walking." Of course, in doing this, you're leaving the problem back in your partner's hands. It's their fight to fight with procurement. You're out of it. And most will then insist that procurement back off of their unreasonable terms and write the contract according to the existing term sheet.

Your goal is to get the procurement department out of the picture as quickly as possible, either by overwhelming them with confusing information or refusing to terms they insist on. As long as you remain on good terms with your business contacts, you can usually get procurement off your back.

Within 60 to 90 days of finalizing a term sheet, you should have an agreement in place. The term sheet shouldn't take more than 30 days to finalize, allowing for time required to get buy-in from marketing, for example. But once that is settled, 60 days are standard for contract approval.

Negotiating an agreement takes time and patience, but as long as you continue to communicate with your partner and explain the rationale for terms that are important to you, it is very likely you can come to agreement. However, never agree to terms that are not advantageous for your business. This is not a short-term sales contract but a long-term business-building partnership. Poor agreements can cause irreparable damage, so enter them carefully.

PART III

KEEPING AN EYE ON THE LONG-TERM POTENTIAL

8

MANAGING STRATEGIC PARTNERS

After countless meetings, the term sheet has been negotiated and signed, the agreement drafted and approved. Now, the real work begins. It is time to execute. You and your sumo now need to determine how to collaborate most effectively to get the best results in the ring. Agreeing to work together on a joint initiative is one thing. Finding a way to get both companies working in concert is a whole new challenge.

One of your first steps at this stage should be to assign an individual to own the relationship. Most companies would assign an account manager to be responsible for the client or customer. This is a sales approach. And a sales account manager with an account management mentality, led by a sales director, is the completely wrong way to go. This is a fatal mistake most companies make.

You don't want account managers. Sales account managers are there to make customers happy, to get reorders. They want to please, which is very easy because the sales relationship is defined by transactions. The people you want for BD are those who will *develop* the partnership. These relationships should always be growing—but not around the transaction. Since one of the most important distinctions between sales and BD is that there is no direct revenue, you should not have someone managing the relationship whose primary focus is revenue. Assigning an individual who will try to grow the relationship by prioritizing transactions will result in failure. We'll talk about the right person for the job in minute.

DEVELOPING PARTNER RELATIONSHIPS

Shortly after starting TrueCar and signing our first enormous sumo, I had a discussion with two of our operations executives. (Both were talented people but are no longer with the company.)

Our discussion topic was a debate over the best way to manage our partnership relationships and, specifically, how we would manage one very large partner that was in the queue for launch. I, of course, am an advocate of keeping the relationships in the BD department. This is what I recommend to anyone running a BD department. This situation is a prime example of why.

John, the vice president of operations, was arguing that his team could handle the entire partner relationship. In this case, the partnership was so large that we were required to have a dedicated employee on staff to manage the operations of the program. The VP claimed that this employee could and should completely manage the relationship.

I challenged him by saying that the role of the relationship manager was different from that of the operations manager. A BD relationship manager, which I refer to as a Partner Development Manager, or PDM, focuses on serving the relationship in order to generate revenue. John replied that he was completely focused on revenue. I said that I believed him, but we were not talking about the same revenue that BD was focused on.

So how can operations and BD be focused on two different revenue sources from the same partner, where operations has to service all revenue, regardless of where or how it comes to the company? To me, it was all about the focus. The revenue was from the same source, but the question was how we got it.

John was right that he and his team were focused on revenue. The partner generated activity, which pushed business through the operational platform that John managed. He was completely focused on how well that platform performed and the resulting revenue. He looked at the performance metrics, which included conversion rates, revenue per transaction, abandon rates, response times, etc. If 10,000 customers came to the business that day, how much money did they generate, and how can we, as a company, make more on those 10,000 customers? That's what John was fixated on. As a BD person, that was exactly what I wanted John and his team focused on.

When I said that the PDM focused on revenue, I was certainly concerned with all that John was working on, but the main focus for the PDM related to the 10,000 customers per day was "How do I grow that to 15,000 per day?" The PDM was concerned with long-term growth. John and his program managers were not thinking that way. Can you see the difference now?

So instead of account or program managers, you want PDMs on your BD team. Their goal is not to sell or to generate direct revenue but to deepen the working relationship you have with the sumos in your corner. Based on that relationship and your strategy for growth, you can crush the competition. However, there are a number of tools you need to have in place to best manage how the partnership functions and flourishes. The first is an "Agenda," with a capital A.

CREATE YOUR AGENDA

At the start of any partnership, you should develop a rolling three-year Agenda. Your Agenda is your list of priorities for the partnership—your road map for where you are going and how you'll leverage your sumo's weight. It is a mini business plan for the initiative from your company's perspective, not something you share with your partner. It addresses high-level questions, such as, "What revenue do you want resulting from this partnership in three years?" "What kind of market leadership will your company enjoy?" "What impact will this partnership have on your company? How will it change as a result?"

Mostly, though, the three-year Agenda is very granular. Why don't you share it with your partner? Because it is just too much information and it contains too many action items. Your PDM will focus on a rolling six-month plan, knowing that at any time, based on the current situation, items from your Agenda are moved off the three-year and onto the six-month plan and vice versa. Your Agenda identifies every possible growth connection you can think of that will help your company achieve its corporate goals (revenue, market share, etc.). This also includes how to make your company critically important to the sumo's business.

Three years is an important time frame because it will take three years for your relationship with your partner to mature. Sure, you will start to see revenue right away and "wins" within three years, but during these first three years, your priorities are different. Your focus during this period will be on (1) developing a strong, collaborative working relationship and (2) looking for ways to achieve smaller wins by leveraging the strategic impact of that partnership. If done well, by year three, the partnership will see significant volume growth from your focus on the first two elements. This growth rate is substantially larger than if you were to push a partner through the prioritization of revenue as the key metric. And with volume comes opportunities to expand the relationship and make even more money.

FORECASTING IN THE DARK

One element of your Agenda that your company and your partner will undoubtedly want to discuss is the revenue forecast. What will this partnership be worth in one, two, three, or five years? Unfortunately, you don't know enough yet about your partner organization, its capabilities, the degree to which it will invest its resources in the project, the speed at which the organization is willing to work. And more importantly, you don't know yet how to prepare a revenue forecast that is based in reality. Sure, you can set goals based on what you would like to have happen. You and your partner should outline those, but the impact they will have on revenue is a complete unknown.

That doesn't mean you should give up on forecasting altogether— far from it. Only realize that your forecast cannot be accurate. You simply don't have enough information. To start, use what you outlined in your agreement as the basis of your forecast. That might include the launch date, when the companies will integrate both technologies, when training of employees will be completed, and how that affects the number of customers you will jointly serve. How much is each customer worth? How quickly will you reach various percentages of your target market? All of those calculations can help you estimate revenue.

Over time, your forecasts will become more accurate. Start by estimating conservatively, to reduce the chance of disappointment on either side, and then readjust after the first few months. By year three, your forecasts should be much more on the mark, based on what you have achieved thus far.

TAKING THE LONG-TERM VIEW

During the first year of your partnership, while you're gearing up for hypergrowth in years two and three, your partner is more concerned about defending their brand and reputation. They are more likely to want to move cautiously forward, testing out your ability to service a subset of their customers before letting you try to service their entire customer base. The sumo's attitude is "Let's just see whether you can handle one of my customers. Don't worry about three years out." They will be monitoring every move you make, confirming that you are doing what you said you would do. You're building trust at this stage, while you take baby steps forward. And yet you, as the BD visionary, have to be looking ahead and planning out three years or you will miss opportunities.

That still does not mean you should share that three-year Agenda with your partner, however. It's frankly too overwhelming to share with them. There are too many elements on it. If you have the ideas and you're leading them down the path, the path that's good for both of you, show them the next few steps on that path—six months out— but no further. They will have difficulty thinking about three years out because the boss is putting pressure on them about their quarterly numbers.

Your Agenda is rolling, because as pieces of the initiative are completed, they fall off the Agenda. As time progresses, you adjust your Agenda and look ahead based on where you are now. And while you are anticipating one, two, and three years ahead, only share the next six months with your sumo. They need to stay tactically focused on the immediate road ahead, while you handle the vision and how your work together will bring that vision to reality.

CONFLICT AND CONTROL
AS YIN AND YANG

As the key contact at the company that conceived the partnership and presented it to the sumo, you may start your relationship in the driver's seat. You're the only person who has the complete picture of what the partnership could look like and mean for both companies, so you are the driving force. That was true as you made pitch after pitch to your partner and did all you could to seal the deal and move forward. But now that you are partners and have a plan of action, the dynamic often shifts. Your partner may want a larger say in how you work together. It is a natural progression in partnerships, but that doesn't mean you should give up control.

The relationship between your two companies will constantly be in flux depending on what is happening with your joint initiative. Where you had more information early on, you had more power. But now that you have outlined a clear path that your two companies will follow, your partner may decide that they want more control. After all, they will tell themselves and you, they know more about their business and their customers than you do, so why shouldn't they be in control of where the partnership is headed? Their confidence and their demand for input and involvement often grow over time.

However, this confidence and desire for complete control are often unjustified. Should they really be allowed to control the direction and course of the partnership? After all, they didn't have the original vision for the venture. Should they be permitted to modify the original plan to better meet their needs? Should their new vision supersede the original project goals? No. In a few cases, the changes sumos demand do enhance the project objectives, but those are the minority. In most cases, their desire for control screws things up.

There are countless examples of partnerships where one party conceives of a grand vision that could benefit both greatly, and then, once the project is under way, the other party decides they know better. Just because your partner has agreed to your vision early on does not mean they will execute it properly. Sure, they may believe that they will, but inserting their own perspective and their own politics and their own limited capabilities or core competencies into the mix impacts the dynamic and the project trajectory. For a variety of reasons, you, as the entrepreneur, have to keep your partner on track.

Because they do not know the ins and outs of your plan the way you do, you cannot relinquish control. If you do, you are allowing the less informed sumo to dictate the project's success. You need to work together, as partners, to achieve the greatest success possible.

Demand for more control will be a routine part of your relationship dynamic. There is no trigger or catalyst you can watch for to sound the alarm that they will soon go offtrack. It will simply happen when your partner begins to feel nervous or uncomfortable with the amount of control you wield. But do not try to avoid these discussions or the conflict that results. Conflict is not a bad thing. Believe it or not, it will help to strengthen your relationship.

Think about it from the perspective of marriage. Dr. John Gottman is the executive director of the Relationship Institute and world renowned for his work on marital stability and divorce predictions. As it relates to conflict, he identifies two different marital styles: conflict engagers and conflict avoiders. Engagers create disagreement but endure short-term unpleasant communication, which is very positive and beneficial to the relationship in the long run. On the other hand, conflict avoidance is dysfunctional and detrimental to the long-term stability of the marriage.

Like marriage, conflict with your sumo is an indicator of a healthy partnership. If no conflict ever erupts, one partner has more power than the other and the relationship is dysfunctional. Conflict is an indicator that you are pushing boundaries and getting each other to think more broadly. It arises from discomfort, but there is no growth without periods of discomfort.

QUESTIONING THE STATUS QUO

Such was the case with one of our partners. We were in year three of a partnership with a very large corporation. In comparison to our nimble entrepreneurial venture, our partner was slow to act. The sumo was big and extremely cautious at every step of the way; it was a cultural thing. They moved at a snail's pace. From the outside, we recognized that the pace did not have to be that way, but people within the organization were so used to lengthy time lines that they couldn't imagine anything else. It was the way they were. However, that pace was not acceptable to us. We were impatient because we knew progress could happen faster.

So when we proposed a next step or a next phase in our partnership, we typically heard something like, "That sounds like a good idea, but you know this organization. That's probably a year away." This was a dialogue that had been going on since the beginning. They truly believed that progress took months, and as a result, their corporate culture limited their growth.

The good news is the company was trying to change. They brought in a new chief executive to shake things up. The people responsible for our initiative, however, still had the old way of thinking. Every idea we pitched was received with, "Gosh, that's great, but it'll take about nine to 12 months to even bring up." Are you kidding?!

Early on, I established a good rapport with the new exec. This wasn't to jump over or alienate our key contact, who was responsible for the day-to-day dealings with our company, but to help him. I knew I needed support to overturn the belief that every step forward would take months and months. So by gaining the backing of senior management, I helped my contact expedite the project. He could no longer say, "It's a nine- to 12-month window to bring it up to management to get it approved," because there had already been dialogue, he didn't have to champion it, and there was already support. So instead of having to wait nearly a year to even ask for approval, we now had approval up front. The team was "allowed" to move forward!

Now when a conversation like the following comes up, here is how I handle it:

> *The client says, "It's going to take nine to 12 months to get that discussion on the table."*
>
> *I respond, "Hold on. That time line doesn't work for us. I see that you like the idea and you want to do it, so what can we do? Let's create this opportunity."*
>
> *He says, "I would love to, but nothing can be done." And he truly believes that. He's not just saying it to try to block the project.*
>
> *So then I pick up the phone and call the executive.*
>
> *Afterward, I let my contact know, telling him, "Just wanted to let you know that I spoke to [let's call him Bob], and we've got the go-ahead to set up this meeting."*
>
> *My contact is not happy at the moment. Does it look like I completely marginalized him? Will I do something to jeopardize his job? Am I going to make him look bad? These are all the things that are running through his mind, which are legitimate concerns. From my perspective, I think I made him look great. We got the approval we were after, and he didn't have to stick his neck out. I really am there to try to help him. I want to make him look like a hero.*

106

This kind of conflict exists at times, and that's OK. In fact, it's good. It often involves pace and progress. But at times, it could be about direction. Keep in mind that conflict does not mean you are in opposition. You can be very much aligned with your partner and still disagree about the details.

Conflict also arises when your partners become so confident of their own capabilities that they decide to make deals on their own, without you. They come to the conclusion that things are going so well that it must be because they are masters at this kind of deal. Why do they need you? they ask themselves. And then the trouble begins.

THE WE-DON'T-NEED-YOU STAGE

We were working with one partner, setting up deals to provide their customers with extra savings on car purchases. We would negotiate with car manufacturers on behalf of our partner to secure savings of $1,000, $2,000, even $5,000 off new car purchases. And then we would pass them along to our partner to benefit their customers.

Then one day they decided things were going so smoothly that they wondered, "How hard can it be to negotiate these deals? We can do this ourselves. We don't need TrueCar." Or at least that's how I imagine the conversation went. So when one car manufacturer stopped calling us and contacted our partner directly to arrange a savings deal, our partner jumped at the opportunity to go it alone. I was livid. And, not surprisingly, it was a terrible deal for their customers and for our partner. I would never have done that deal.

So I told them, "If you think you can put these deals together yourself, I'm not having another conversation with a manufacturer about you again. We're not bringing you any more value." They agreed, but unfortunately, that did not hold for long. In an identical situation a few weeks later, we were in discussions with a manufacturer that decided to see whether they could work directly with our partner. Our partner attempted to structure another deal without much success. After 18 months, they were no further along in the negotiations than when they started.

At the same time, there was an executive change. The new exec, who had been involved in our partnership and was a friend, was now promoted to lead our relationship. He wanted to do the right thing and asked that we get involved in structuring this deal. But, in this case, I stuck to my word. Since we were previously cut out of the opportunity, I would not get involved to help close this deal. This was a principle issue for me, and it became a major friction point in our relationship.

In the meantime, we were still arranging great deals for other companies. And our divisive partner saw this. There was even more conflict between us. So they came back to us, and I told them, in no uncertain terms, "You have treated us so poorly that I am reluctant to talk about you and your company to anyone again. So if you want to partner with us again, you have to agree, contractually now, that we are together on this initiative. That doesn't mean that you're not involved in the conversations; it just means that you're not going to undermine our efforts. If you can agree to that, then we can start again."

Fortunately, my executive friend inherited this situation. It wasn't his forte and he knew, through direct experience, that we were the subject matter experts. He thought it best if we worked out the savings terms with car manufacturers. We are good at it. This is why the car manufacturers tried to cut us out of the opportunity in the first place, to try to take advantage of our partners. I then educated him about how the deals they did without us had loopholes that were bad for their customers. They knew they had made a major error. However, having cut us out of the deals and then realizing the error of their ways, they now appreciate us that much more. The conflict that arose ultimately strengthened our relationship and our partnership. We are now united moving forward, and while other disagreements will come up in the future, it won't be around this issue.

ARE YOU IN THE FRONT SEAT OR THE BACK SEAT?

What makes a partnership different from a vendor-client relationship is that both companies have a stake in the initiative. Both are decision makers. Yet some BD pros forget that. I was having a conversation with a good CEO friend of mine; he's a smart guy and totally understands BD and how it works. Unfortunately, he was not paying enough attention to the partner management skills of his team and, subsequently, was not getting the results he expected from his sumo.

I had introduced him to one of our partners a couple of years before. I was sure there was an opportunity to do something with this partner. A deal was cut between them with the potential for a material impact on the company's revenue and long-term enterprise value. When I caught up with the CEO more than a year later, I asked how his deal was working out with our mutual partner. "Are you in growth mode yet?" I asked. Remember it takes three years to mature a partner and he was two years in.

"No, not really," he told me, "but next year we will be. The partner has some hurdles to overcome before we can take the next step. They're a major corporation, and we are in 'wait' mode. Nothing we can do!"

I was dumbfounded. How is it that the CEO of a respected company, and a person I think is brilliant in BD, would essentially throw his hands up in the air and say, "What can we do?!"

I was blown away that he couldn't figure out how to create the conflict and the urgency within the relationship. Instead, he completely empowered them. His company sat back and waited for the sumo to make a move. He left it completely up to them to decide how, when, and whether they would move forward with the Agenda. I suspected that whoever was managing the partner had a problem with conflict. In this person's mind, it was wait or express displeasure with the situation, which he or she clearly wasn't personally comfortable doing.

When companies put the brakes on progress, saying that their process takes X months, you have to let them know that there needs to be a change. You have to say, "Wait—that's not OK for my business, but, more importantly, it's not OK for our collective customers. We're partners and we need to move forward on other action items while we wait for the big initiative to kick in." Some things you can't speed up, such as a planned marketing campaign, but there are plenty of other things you can do in the meantime to try to pick up volume.

After our discussion, my CEO friend decided to set up an all-day meeting with his sumo. He spent the entire day inserting conflict into the discussion. At the end of the day, he had deepened the relationship. The two parties worked through the challenges, and through my buddy's facilitation, did not let anyone "kick the can down the road" on any given issue. So now, while they are still waiting for the big action item to launch, he cleared a path to grow revenue by 40 percent and help hundreds of thousands of new customers. He also fired his PDM the following day.

My point here is that managing a sumo is not easy and even seasoned BD professionals can stumble. I certainly have. But you can be assured that with the right tactics and through healthy conflict, you will certainly get the partnership back on track and on its way to prosperity.

Part of the approach to drive commitment may be a conversation that goes something like this:

> *"OK, so the plan is Q3 of next year, we're going to launch*
> *a TV advertising campaign. So here's what I want to*

do before that to make sure we get the most benefit from
that TV campaign. What we need is more water run-
ning through the pipes **now** *to test value propositions X,*
Y, and Z."

Now you're getting some alignment. You're explaining what you can do now to support your sumo's future TV campaign. You're not trying to push ahead with anything. You're trying to enhance the results achieved through this other event. Instead of doing nothing, you're doing something in preparation for the other goal, which they are, in a sense, in control of. And you're creating a reason for why there's urgency now—for the impending event that's coming. As long as you're aligning with their goals, you should be able to create more urgency or demand now. It's never, ever OK, unless there's some catastrophe, to just go, "Well, we just have to sit and wait."

This is true unless you absolutely have to sit and wait because you truly have no other alternative. Once in a while, situations arise that bring initiatives to a standstill. We had a great partnership with a major credit card company, but when they got hit with a near-$100-million fine, we had to stop what we were doing together, even though the fine was unrelated to our partnership. All of their resources had to be redirected to addressing policy modifications due to that massive fine, rather than pursuing growth through a BD partnership. It was a temporary situation that we, as their partner, needed to support.

KEEPING THE FOCUS
OFF SHORT-TERM ROI

Since BD projects are not sales initiatives, odds are good that your investment will not pay off in year one. And that is fine. BD is a longer-term process that involves building the relationship first and looking for strategic value for both partners second. If you do those first two things well, revenue will result automatically. You can't rush revenue generation. If you do, it will be at the expense of the relationship or the strategic impact, both key to your ultimate success.

Sales, on the other hand, is completely focused on the short-term return on investment (ROI). Success in sales is based on revenue now. It's all about the transaction, not the relationship. BD pros are much more willing to forgo revenue today to set the partners up for greater success in the coming months and years.

MAKING A TRUE COMMITMENT TO BD

There are times when you have to convince your own company to do something in support of your BD initiative. In many cases, the effort to gain their support can be as great as negotiating with an outside partner.

The challenge you inevitably face is in obtaining support for an initiative that will not generate revenue this year. Most companies are focused on managing this year's budget. Seeing resources being committed without a near-term ROI can be troubling to them. You need balance. If the company is fixated on driving revenue this year, your chances of BD success drop dramatically. Both companies have to commit to supporting the joint initiative for a minimum of two to three years. Only at that point will you have a better assessment of the long-term revenue potential. As I always say, the company priorities are focused on revenue this year, but BD delivers what the company will focus on next year.

9

THE BEST PARTNER
DEVELOPMENT
MANAGERS (PDMS)

Strong Partner Development Managers (PDMs) can make or break a relationship with a sumo. For that reason, you need great ones on your team—good just won't cut it. And make no mistake: the skills a PDM needs are quite different from the skills a sales account manager needs. You don't need an order taker or someone who is "ready to please," who has a "customer-is-always-right" attitude. You need a persuasive mini entrepreneur—someone who expands relationships to transform both companies.

Effective PDMs are tough yet flexible; those that are weak are easy prey for the sumo who will flip them over and move the situation from partnership to vendor in mere seconds. They need to be resourceful and creative, hungry and competitive, unwilling to give up. Yet they need to be patient, pushy only when opportunities that benefit the sumo will soon be lost. They need to be more focused on the relationship than the revenue to be generated. But most of all, they need to be willing to embrace conflict as a tool. BD deals are more like joint ventures that are governed by expanding and exploiting a collective opportunity.

You aren't a vendor selling a product or service—you are an equal working to benefit both companies. In this case, the PDM is more like the coach to the mighty sumo—there to lead them to victory for both of your sakes.

Keep in mind that sumos aren't used to having partners in the ring with them. They are generally loners who are quite capable of fighting their own fights, so having to take into account a partner's needs and requests could be a new experience for them. PDMs need to be able to inform, educate, and inspire, without patronizing or backing down.

That's a long list of must-haves, I realize. Yet there are capable, talented businesspeople who are more than able to step into those shoes. Unfortunately, you may need to weed out some of the sales account managers in order to find your star PDM.

IDENTIFYING THE PARTNER DEVELOPMENT SUPERSTARS

Finding your superstar is not easy, and I say that based on personal experience. I'm very careful about whom I hire, but sometimes even people with the best résumés, recommendations, and interviews slip through. It may even take several months before you realize they aren't doing what you hired them to do. That was the case with one guy I hired from Yahoo. He understood the importance of a good working partner relationship and was certainly focused on building that. But he was a people pleaser—he wanted the partner to love him. That was more important to him than anything else, and the sumo quickly caught on. He became the sumo's assistant in many ways, rather than the coach.

Accordingly, the sumo dictated all time lines and repeatedly asked for things from him knowing that he would bend over backward to accommodate their requests. Did they always make sense? No. But he was too busy keeping them happy to evaluate the requests to determine whether it made sense for us to fulfill them. What finally tipped me off to the imbalance in our relationship with the sumo was when we would ask for something simple, which would benefit both companies, and yet they didn't have time to even consider the request. The partner didn't listen to him, didn't take him seriously, and would hear his words but not act on any of his requests. As a result, I had to let him go. He couldn't be effective in a PDM role.

Another seemingly good hire that went bad also had a great relationship with one of our partners. She understood what she was expected to do and was excellent at nurturing the relationship but had no idea how to get around obstacles that came up. She couldn't get the partner to agree to any condition that might be in the slightest way "risky" or "aggressive," even when it would be extremely beneficial to both parties. Being so limited in what we could do meant that we couldn't ever generate the volume the partnership had the potential to. PDMs have to help partners see that while some decisions could be slightly difficult in the short term, there are significant long-term gains that would make it worthwhile. She wasn't capable, so I had to let her go, too.

What they had in common, which is what made them attractive PDM candidates, was their commitment to building and nurturing partner relationships. They truly believed that a good relationship was tantamount to success, and it is. Where they fell short was in not embracing conflict as a tool to better the relationship. They were afraid to have a confrontation for fear that it would jeopardize their number-one goal of getting the partner to "love" them. But getting the sumo to love them was not their job, and it was not the goal. In these cases, I prefer that the partner respect the PDM over loving the PDM. You are not hiring ass kissers. What you want are "ass kickers" that understand how to build a relationship through respect, trust, and a thorough demonstration of competence.

I'm tough, and I know many partners have felt that way about me at one point or another. But they also know that I never have and never will steer them in a direction that is purely selfish or detrimental to them. Our disagreement is never about the goal but the method to achieving that goal. That's where healthy debate and, yes, conflict, come into play. What I view as healthy conflict others may view as fighting or being difficult. Make sure your PDMs subscribe to the former; otherwise, I can guarantee two things: (1) the partnership will not realize its potential and (2) you will wind up firing the PDM once you realize this.

In addition to being diplomats and negotiators, the best PDMs are entrepreneurs at heart. They like being in control of and responsible for revenue-generating opportunities and relationships. To do that, they stay in close contact with partners and all employees active in the partnership. They are involved in any discussions that affect the partner, to avoid conflicts or decisions that negatively affect either company. In addition to serving as partner representative, they also are the point person, but not a bottleneck, for the project as a whole, alerting both companies about challenges that may soon arise. Anticipating issues makes it possible to more effectively assess and plan, rather than operating in crisis mode when a challenge appears that no one was prepared for. With all that they have to manage, they are very much like an entrepreneur, leading the partnership and trying to capitalize on every possible revenue-generating initiative, while being personally responsible for every decision made.

PROFILE OF A
SUCCESSFUL HIRE

Experience running his own clothing company, which he grew from tens of thousands to hundreds of thousands of dollars in a few short years, was what made David Pributsky an attractive PDM candidate at TrueCar six years ago. He had been responsible for revenue, forged partnerships with local sumos, and experienced the give and take necessary to be a successful business owner. That entrepreneurial background made him a standout because he had already successfully managed and grown his own venture. Transferring that experience to BD at TrueCar would be fairly simple.

Now, as vice president of partner development, Pributsky is a master of partner relationships. He recognizes that he can't be a total pleaser but tries to say yes when it is necessary or possible. He often finds that what partners ask for isn't necessarily what they need; it may be what they *think* they need to address a particular problem, however. Pributsky finds himself using the following sentence quite frequently as he tries to find out what the partner really needs: "I know you're saying *this*, but I think you mean *that*."

Understanding the partner's goals and needs is crucial for success as a PDM, he says. Through his work at another company, Pributsky got to know the major players in the auto industry, putting him in good position to advance TrueCar's plans for growth. Familiarity with the industry helped him understand what industry products and systems were in use, as well as where the weaknesses and opportunities were.

Another successful hire at TrueCar is Jason Nierman, who has worked with TrueCar for more than five years, initially as a BD hunter. Before entering the automotive industry, Nierman worked in consulting and marketing and public relations. Now, as vice president of partner development, his responsibilities include motivating partners and his team to expand the partnerships by aligning TrueCar's services with each partner's core products, rather than simply using the company's offering as an add-on benefit.

Being aggressive and being comfortable pushing partners— challenging their views when appropriate—are two traits Nierman believes are necessary for success in BD. Partners need to know, like, and trust a PDM in order to bring important projects to fruition. Nierman also believes resourcefulness is key; you need to be able to "leverage your bench," or your colleagues and internal champions, to push initiatives forward. Good PDMs make nearly all decisions regarding partners on their own, but they also know when to bring in the big guns, he explains.

ASSESSING POTENTIAL FOR SUCCESS AS A PDM

It can be difficult to assess a candidate's fit for a PDM position, especially if he or she has a sales background or no BD experience. I've found the candidate evaluation approach shared in the book *Topgrading*, by Bradford D. Smart, to be extremely useful. In fact, I have developed my own take on some of the questions, which I have adapted specifically for PDM interviews.

RIGHT FIT

- What does your ideal position look like, and why is it ideal for you? [Listen for whether the candidate has passion in what you know he or she will need to do, versus what he or she describes.]
- If we invite you to join our company, what would you do first?
- Would you say you are more of a visionary or an implementer?

- What do you consider to be challenges or obstacles at work, and how do you typically work around them?
- Give me an example of a challenge you faced on a recent project.
- What experience have you had in strategic planning? Give me an example of a plan or project that worked and one that did not go as planned and why.

ASSERTIVENESS AND CONFLICT

- Give me an example of when you disagreed with your boss. What was the disagreement about, and how did you approach your boss?
- How would you handle a situation where your partner or spouse thinks he or she has a great idea and you think it would be bad?
- Are you more likely to prevent a conflict from erupting or help resolve it once it has emerged?
- What are some examples of major risks you've recently taken? How did they turn out, and why do you think you got the result you did?
- Have you ever been in a situation where you were pressured to compromise your integrity? How did you handle it?
- Describe a situation where you have taken an unpopular stance. What happened?
- Are you more likely to obtain agreement and approval from your boss before proceeding, or are you in position to do what makes the most sense to you and ask forgiveness later?
- How do you typically handle differences of opinion? Are you more likely to confront someone directly, approach him or her indirectly, or avoid the situation until it blows over?

119

- What kind of results do you typically achieve when you are assertive? Do you get what you want? Has there ever been a situation where your assertiveness backfired?
- How do you navigate corporate politics?
- What are some recent situations involving company politics that you found difficult or challenging to deal with?
- Have you ever been in a situation where you were certain you were right and others were wrong? What did you do about it? How did it resolve?
- Can you describe a recent example of where you helped foster cooperation and teamwork?

Relationship Building and Management

- Could you provide an example of how you partnered with a client to help them achieve their goals or improve their financial performance?
- Have you ever been in a situation where you had trouble maintaining your emotional composure? Describe it.
- Have you ever had to work with someone you didn't like? What was that like? How did you get past your personal feelings and still be productive?
- How effectively would your coworkers say you are at using active listening?
- What would your clients say are your strengths and weaknesses?
- Tell me about a time when a client was extremely disappointed with you. Did you agree with their assessment of the situation?
- Tell me about a time when your negotiating skills were helpful. And how about a time when they were not?
- Have you ever broken a confidence? What was the situation?

- Describe a time when you proactively asserted yourself to improve your company's image or the perception clients had of it.

Through the candidate's responses to these questions, you should be able to gauge how comfortable he or she is with creating and managing conflict, nurturing relationships without becoming a yes-man or yes-woman, and whether his or her experience and goals match where you're taking your company.

WHY A SPIDEY SENSE IS SO IMPORTANT

In addition to confidence and relationship-building skills, the best PDMs also have what I call a "Spidey Sense," a commonality shared with Spiderman. That sixth sense is essentially intuition and intimate familiarity with a partner that tells you when something's up. PDMs who have a strong Spidey Sense know when they have enough support in the room to push for a contract, and they also instinctively know when to back down.

That Spidey Sense, like when the hairs on the back of your neck stick up, warns you when something is off with a partner—maybe they're trying to negotiate something behind your back and are exuding a guilty vibe, maybe they learned they're not going to be able to come through for you on something you asked for but they don't yet have the courage to admit it, or maybe they are heading into the overconfidence spiral that can cause your project to go off track. A Spidey Sense will shine a spotlight on extra hostility between two senior execs, or one leader's sudden desire to repeatedly change the subject when you ask for a favor, or the general lively mood in the room, suggesting now would be a good time to ask for something. It's part perceptiveness, part empathy, and part observation all rolled into one.

Spidey Sense proves quite useful when sumos start entering the cycle of confidence—that phase when they see the results that are possible and believe that they are more meaningful to a successful partnership than you are. After all, they are the major force in their industry, they will tell themselves, and how much value can you truly be providing, they will often ask themselves. When your Spidey Sense starts tingling, it's a warning that conflict is coming. This occurs regularly, and PDMs who can sense when a partner is starting down this path can help get them back on track before any damage is done.

Imagine you are the lead PDM. You are great at leveraging conflict for the greater good of the partnership, and you are managing a partner that frequently tries to do what they want for their own good, believing that you, as a partner, should act like a vendor.

As a great PDM, you are an ambassador for them within your company, as well as an advocate for your company with a strong three-year Agenda. While always involved, you are never a bottleneck and ensure that direct discussions between your company's resources and your partner's flows, but with supervision. It is well known that you must always be on calls involving modifications or difficult discussions; you've all agreed to that.

Let's look at an example. One day, you hear from your team that your contacts have scheduled a meeting with a few people but chose not to include you. Your Spidey Sense starts to tingle. "That's odd," you think to yourself. You recall some of the conversations you have recently had with your partner and conclude, "Something's not right." So you ask your team to send you the conference line information.

Sure enough, the call erupts into the partner asking for what would normally appear to be a small technical change. In most cases, a tech person on your side might just process the request. In this case, you jump in and head it off at the pass. The request involved making a change to the website you don't agree with. "Absolutely not!" is your answer. In your mind, lawyers don't run the business, but to your very large partner, lawyers have more power than most employees. They are thinking they have to take their lawyers' advice, and you are standing your ground. This type of change has the potential to negatively impact the site's performance metrics, so this change must have some major justification, and, in your experience, there is none.

Your Spidey Sense kicked in at the right time. Many would have just let the conference call proceed with the invitees, and, in some cases, that is fine. In this case, the PDM knew—actually felt—that something was not right.

In the book *Path to the Entreprenati*, the author, Pace Klein, talks about the sensing self. In our case, your "path" refers to your partner and the three-year Agenda, and, as Klein puts it, "It is changing all along the way. We're talking about achieving a state of awareness in which you're tuned into this interaction between you and your path—its effect on you, and its effect on your path."

A PDM's ability to sense the potential for problems and take back control of the discussion is one of the defining attributes for increasing your chances of a fruitful partnership.

PDMs who have an innate Spidey Sense are like gold, because they will be far more successful at building relationships and negotiating deliverables from the get-go. They'll also have a higher degree of accuracy in establishing milestone time lines and moving them along. But that doesn't mean you can't help them develop it. Many PDMs have all the skills necessary but haven't yet learned how to leverage them.

One of the best ways to build a Spidey Sense is by studying how the members of a partner's team interact with each other and with members of your team. During a meeting, how do they initiate discussions about a difficult topic? Is there a designated deliverer of bad news? Do they change personalities when a senior executive attends a meeting? Monitor their body language for clues regarding their overall attitude. What kinds of side chatter can you pick up that provide additional tidbits about what's going on behind the scenes?

Once you know how people react in certain settings—say, a planning session or when including the technology department—you can more easily compare how they act or react in a situation where tension is present. Seeing and recognizing the clues are the start of developing a valuable Spidey Sense.

SCALING PARTNER MANAGEMENT

It's one thing to get a partnership, and it's quite another to build an entire strategy around BD activity. Scaling this initiative is not a simple endeavor. The key is finding and organizing a team of the right people. So how do you know whether you have the right people?

Even within BD, there are different roles. There are BD hunters, and there are PDMs. The hunters are not the PDMs. You can start with one person playing a dual role on your first and even second deal, but it won't hold beyond that. These are two different roles, and the hunter can handle the partner development activities, but he or she will eventually need to hand it off. Initially, the (post-agreement) partnership will still require the evangelic pitch to get the rest of the group on board. There is no better person to do this than the person who built the relationship with the original business champions, generally the hunter. The hunter will need to leverage the relationship to get past the initial obstacles. Perhaps you want a press release issued and the partner is not ready until the pilot phase is completed. Or you want the nationwide marketing blitz to start but some manager on the partner side thinks you should launch locally first. The PDM is generally not the most effective when conflict arises in the first 90 days.

That's why the ideal scenario for scaling the initiative is to follow the PDM Transition Flow, which you can find at BernieBrenner.com. In this process, the PDM is included close to when the term sheet is completed but certainly before the relationship moves into the agreement phase. This is a critical relationship-building technique so that the hunter can effectively hand off the relationship much sooner.

You may recall that the agreement phase is where the lawyers get involved to help memorialize the term sheet. The business owner has already agreed to a variety of terms, but some will still be challenged at the contract level. While you should anticipate getting agreement as you did with the term sheet, some items could be very painful for the business owner and for the company. You want the PDM to know just how difficult those terms were to swallow. The PDM should be connected to the process in order to respect the situation. By no means is this to suggest that the PDM may back down from what is needed or agreed to. Rather, there's a difference between saying "What's the date of the press release?" and saying "I know getting the press release approved prior to the pilot was a difficult component to agree to and will most likely be tough to work on internally within your company. But given that we did agree, I would like us to begin the process so we can drop it in the next couple of weeks. What can I do to help you?"

As the agreement is moving forward, the PDM begins to rally the internal resources in anticipation of an eventual agreement. Resources are not allocated at this point, but the opportunity is being evaluated for the development and launch queues.

During the kickoff meeting, you'll want your first-year goals defined, as well as the marketing plan necessary to achieve those goals. At this stage, the give and take really flourishes as your sumo tries to avert resource costs until the perceived risk has been mitigated.

Generally, in the sumo's mind, this risk is associated with time. In time, they can see how good your company is at what it says it does. In time, customers will share their experience with the product or service. In time, the sumo can assess how much money they have available to fund resource development. This is where your BD hunter or brilliant PDM finesses an accelerated scenario. Left alone, the sumo will move slowly, as they have other opponents to deal with in their own battle ring. That's not OK with you. You need their resources for your battle ring, and as an entrepreneur fighting to grow your business, patience is not one of your virtues, nor should it be.

When you finally launch, the initial 60 days are critical. Consider this the learning phase where you are preparing for your first round of optimizations. During this time, you and your sumo are working on what to do next, and you, as in every other case, are leading the discussion. You want this sumo to get aggressive, and in the back of your mind, you are always thinking about how to use the partnership to grow your partner's core business. Once that is achieved, the sumo will jump into warrior mode, kicking the crap out of their competition and helping you do the same with yours.

One final tip on scaling the initiative: the hunter transitions back to hunting, while the PDM develops the ongoing relationship. But the hunter still maintains a relationship, in the background, through the term of the agreement. This is another critical point because the hunter may be needed when new negotiations come up. If you and your partner are expanding or changing the terms, don't have the PDM negotiate this. It's very easy to think that since the PDM has the ongoing relationship, then the PDM can handle it all. I don't agree.

The PDM should never be put in a position where he or she is sitting on the opposite side of the table. New negotiations related to terms do just that. Even when the PDM is dealing with intense conflict with the partner, it is always for the greater good of the partnership, and, therefore, the PDM and the partner are still sitting on the same side of the table.

BEST PRACTICES

The best PDMs—the most effective at bringing in deals and keeping partners engaged for the long term—are able to focus on the relationship, first and foremost, without allowing the pressure to generate revenue supersede that. Sales account managers often run into this problem—the rush to generate revenue—where PDMs understand that by investing time and energy to build a relationship, revenue will eventually result.

The most talented PDMs are generally *not* former sales reps. It's difficult to transform someone who has been trained to go for the yes and get the immediate sale to back off, try not to get a no, and put aside revenue generation as the short-term goal. Instead, look for former entrepreneurs who have lived with that balance. Their skills and experiences are likely to be a better match for the talent you need to grow your company.

10

THE BD-CENTRIC ORGANIZATION

It can be hard to transition from a typical sales-oriented organization, where the focus is on doing what's best for the company *now*, to a BD-centric company, which looks ahead to what's best for the company *in the future*. You might think that these dual goals are always aligned, but often they are not. The goals for next quarter or next year may actually be diametrically opposed to the goals for five years from now, and this dichotomy can cause a lot of friction internally. That was certainly the case when I was at Carfax several years ago.

Carfax wanted dealers to run more reports. That was their goal. At the time, car dealers typically ran a small number of Carfax reports a month, relative to the fleet of 50 to 75 cars they had on the lot at the time. To access the information, they logged in to the dealer portal at Carfax.com and entered the car's 17-digit vehicle identification number (VIN). Once the VIN was typed in, they could run a report detailing the vehicle's ownership and maintenance and repair history. However, the process was cumbersome and time consuming if the dealer was trying to generate reports on multiple vehicles at once. The system worked and the company was meeting its goals, but the customer (the dealer) had a difficult time using this "properly working system."

The BD team recommended moving forward with an integration strategy, merging the Carfax capabilities with any system that a dealer already used to store VINs so they wouldn't have to reenter them. If they had an inventory management system, for example, all they would have to do is click a button to run a report.

The decision to pursue dealer integration was a carefully calculated strategic move. Although such a step would require an allocation of resources to complete, we knew it would help grow the business. We needed our system to be easier to use—a one-click process—in order to grow. So we proceeded with our first integration, which was a relatively small project. Looking ahead, the BD team saw its potential.

The chief technology officer (CTO), however, did not. He questioned why the company was even pursuing integration at all. He pointed out that the current deal generated a miniscule 0.00024 percent of revenue—nearly nothing, comparatively. Proceeding with integration plans certainly wouldn't generate substantial revenue this year, so he was against it. He wanted the allocation of resources to this initiative stopped, immediately. Clearly, he had a sales mind-set.

Fortunately, Carfax's CEO and senior management had a BD mind-set. They knew the CTO was dead wrong about the potential revenue to be generated from future partnerships. They also recognized that this was a pivotal moment for the company, and they were behind their BD team. We had completed one small integration project and had at least 50 major ones out there still to be done. We proceeded with the integration with the anticipation that it would positively impact revenue in the future—not in the next year but two or three years hence.

We were right. Two years later, we had all the remaining integration deals under way. A year after that, the majority of Carfax's revenue could be tied back to the system integration. The average number of reports run by dealers each month had climbed substantially. But it hadn't happened overnight. Only because the company had made BD a priority and had committed to the long-term vision was this a success. Many companies aren't as lucky, unfortunately.

That is not to say that technology and operations-focused professionals don't have their place, however. It is the CTO's job and the chief operating officer's (COO's) job to question how you as a company are allocating resources. They are the keepers of the short-term vision. They are responsible for doing as much as possible with the limited resources available today. And if the CTO or COO didn't stop and question some of your decisions, they wouldn't be doing their jobs effectively. That said, in a BD-centric organization, they should not have the power to halt such initiatives, either.

THE SUCCESSFUL BD MIND-SET

The natural inclination for organizations is to focus on ROI-positive efforts, meaning ROI positive *now*—not next year or the year after but this year. Unfortunately, that outlook is inconsistent with BD efforts. You can't be BD oriented and plan for your partnerships to generate revenue in the near term. They won't, mainly because that is not how they are structured. BD partnerships are multiyear projects. Focusing on revenue as the primary objective will doom BD efforts to failure. Said another way, you will earn the least amount of revenue from the partnership if you make revenue generation the priority.

BD partnerships are initiatives designed to make all involved lots of money if things go as planned. And that's a big *if.* Most of the time partners can align their strategies, but the actual execution of those strategies does not always go as expected. And, let's be honest, the majority of BD initiatives don't succeed on the scale that the partners had hoped.

The main problem with these unsuccessful ventures is the lack of a BD mind-set. Companies that understand the value that a BD Layer brings to the organization as a whole recognize that BD has the power to accelerate sales exponentially. The key sticking point is whether the organization can wait.

Early on, BD requires an investment. You need people dedicated to pursuing BD deals, you need resources allocated internally to execute tasks on behalf of partners, and you need sufficient finances to allow the company to continue to operate while you identify revenue-generating opportunities. Without that commitment, pursuing successful BD deals will be an uphill battle.

Additionally, your partner at some point may ask for support in a way that is not ROI positive for you. Maybe they need a technology capability that you already possess but that they don't want to pay for or they need you to build out a certain functionality for the platform you're working off of. In a sales organization, the knee-jerk reaction will typically be to say no unless money changes hands. But this isn't a sales transaction. You're building equity in your partnership, and it may cost you up front. Every task associated with the project may not be ROI positive, and that's OK. If you know it is in the best interests of the partnership, don't dismiss the request without a lot of discussion. Taking a small financial hit here could be a turning point in your relationship with your partner.

THE PDM AS LIAISON

The main responsibility for supporting a BD mind-set belongs to senior management. Sure, PDMs are responsible for executing the

BD plan—conceiving of revenue-generating partnerships, identifying potential organizations to partner with, selling the vision, negotiating the agreement, and then pushing the objectives forward once the deal is signed. But senior management needs to make it clear to the rest of the organization what their priorities are. If this has been done, the PDM's job becomes much simpler.

When management backs BD initiatives, there is less push back when a partner asks for something that is ROI negative. If the company is structured to encourage and support projects involving sumos, there should be little internal campaigning or negotiating necessary when a PDM decides approving a partner's request is in everyone's best interest. After all, if you've carefully selected a PDM who has all the qualities necessary to be successful, you need to trust that he or she has accurately assessed the situation.

On the other hand, if you force a PDM to justify every request for support, the project will grind to a halt while you second-guess the person who's actually in the ring with the sumo. That person is in the ring to create alignment and to leverage the sumo's strengths to address your company's competitive needs.

What you want to do is minimize the amount of effort the PDM has to exert to get his or her own company to support the initiative. It's hard enough to get the other company to continuously support the initiative, especially when they're the sumo, who naturally does not align with anyone, is big, and is focused on beating up the competition.

Demanding justification for a BD request is, in most cases, a complete waste of time for everyone involved. You really need to trust that your PDM is your first line of defense; if the PDM is asking for support on a particular task, he or she probably already turned down three or four other prior requests the sumo made. Many sumos will ask for things simply because it could benefit them in some way and they know it won't cost them anything. Smart PDMs know to turn those down immediately or only occasionally to quote a price for the extra work. But just as frequently, your partner may make a request that makes sense and that deserves attention. If it solves a problem for them and won't cost you much to deliver, you should do it. You'll build equity in the relationship bank account that will be there for you to withdraw later. These requests are opportunities worthy of attention. Remember that the PDM's Agenda prioritization order is (1) relationship, (2) strategic impact, and (3) revenue.

Give your PDM the respect he or she deserves by approving these requests without much difficulty. It's more than likely that he or she has already weighed the pros and cons and is taking the long-term view in making the request. Trust in your PDM.

With the right PDM in place, you're well positioned to land and leverage sumo partners. When you find someone who is a strong relationship builder and a good communicator, who is comfortable creating and managing conflict to grow the partnership, who can prioritize and stick to an agenda, and who possesses a Spidey Sense that tips him or her off to coming relationship challenges, your odds of success are high.

DEFENSIVE STRATEGIZING CREATES OPPORTUNITIES

Part of being a BD-oriented organization means routinely identifying opportunities to partner. My preferred way to do this is to consider how our competitors could really clobber us in the marketplace. What could they do to damage our current and future revenue streams? When we at TrueCar asked that question back in 2008, we uncovered a huge opportunity.

We were working with a few membership-based direct auto lenders at the time to help their members buy cars. A direct lender arranges financing for applicants, who can then turn around and buy from any auto dealer of their choosing. At the same time, auto dealers offer to facilitate auto loans, which is referred to as indirect lending, as an alternative option for customers who want to buy a car. In many cases, and especially when you have been turned down by a direct lender for their absolutely lowest rate, the dealer can be your best option for finding the most competitive financing. TrueCar was working with these affinity lenders to provide members with exclusive rebates and savings, connecting auto manufacturers, dealers, and consumers. The three-party relationship was going well. And then came the financial crash of September 2008.

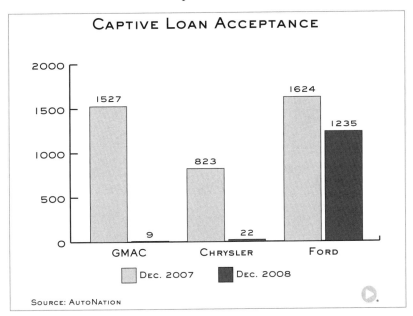

Credit dried up, with most lenders and dealers hit particularly hard from their indirect lender partners. Mike Jackson, the chairman and CEO of AutoNation, which is America's largest automotive retailer, presented the above slide at a conference. It was one of the most revealing insights into the challenges dealerships faced during the fourth quarter of 2008.

135

As you can see, the financial arms of the Big Three auto manufacturers faced their own challenges, with two of the three virtually denying all applications. These lenders, in particular, exist solely for the purpose of helping their parent companies, GM, Chrysler, and Ford, sell more vehicles. Yet in December of 2008, GMAC helped AutoNation sell nine cars compared with 1,527 in the same period the year before. Chrysler Financial went from 823 loans in December 2007 to 22 loans in December 2008. Unless customers came in with cash in hand or financing from other sources, dealers couldn't sell cars. Dealers had cars on their lots that weren't moving, so they started to cut back on all advertising—TV, newspaper, and online subscription advertising services that theoretically competed with TrueCar. However, what dealerships across the country weren't cutting back on were their fees to TrueCar.

We became even more important to our dealers. Through our partnerships, TrueCar was one of the few sources of pre-financed customers these dealers had. Regardless of what was happening in the market, we were busy. Using strategic partners allowed us to keep that flywheel spinning, even when other things were disruptive. While dealers were cutting expenses related to advertising, they weren't cutting TrueCar because many of our customers were still buying cars. It was a total winner for them.

BD-centric organizations are much more likely to be composed of innovators and big-picture thinkers. They envision partnerships that can disrupt the market and solidify their place as leaders. Your BD Layer will help grow your business in the good times but also sustain your business in the bad times. Like the dealer community at the end of 2008, relying on your next financeable customer to walk through the door jeopardized the business, and, as a result, thousands of dealers shut their doors. We are all vulnerable to these market uncertainties, and BD plays a major role in your company's sustainability, growth, and enterprise value.

136

11

STRATEGIC THINKING— LEVERAGE YOUR KILLER APP

The following may or may not apply to your particular business. Either way, however, you should still find this very helpful, as it will certainly enhance your thinking related to the strategic landscape of your business or industry. In many cases, I believe an entrepreneurial company can leverage its killer app once its executives know what to look for. And what becomes your killer app does not start as one. It starts as an idea around how to cement your position in the market. We all want that.

The term "killer app" has evolved in the past few years from a reference to a software application to a more general term for a unique corporate capability that moves the market in your direction. A killer app is a functionality that forces the market to adopt your company's product or service. Its mere existence boxes out the competition. Killer apps are game changers, capable of pushing your opponent out of the ring altogether.

Facebook Connect is a quintessential example of a killer app. Connect is actually a widget that allows Facebook users to log in to other websites and applications quickly and easily using their Facebook login information. Rather than having to type in a separate user ID and password, people can simply use their Facebook ID to access newspapers, entertainment websites, or special promotions and money-saving coupons. Connect is a gateway for users and for companies that want access to the vast amounts of consumer data Facebook collects. Connect is a killer app because many consumers have a Facebook account, it is easier to get adoption by using Facebook as the log-in device, and companies that use it get useful consumer insights from Facebook. Coupled with first-mover advantage, which is the advantage companies can earn by being the first major player in a space, Connect will be hard to displace, much like a skilled sumo.

Connect is Facebook's killer app because its existence makes it that much harder for Facebook to be overthrown as the sumo of social networks. Without Connect, Facebook is just another social network, much like MySpace or Badoo. But because of Connect's single sign-in functionality, Facebook is much more than a destination for connecting with friends. Consumers are finding the convenience of single sign-in through their Facebook account to be preferable to remembering a slew of other usernames and passwords. The evidence? As of Q1 2013, Facebook owned 46 percent of the social sign-in market, with Google+ in second, at 34 percent. On the business-to-business side, Facebook is now the backbone on which a tremendous amount of data sits, thanks to Connect. An increasing number of companies have become reliant on that data that Connect provides about users who sign in to other sites using their Facebook account. Thanks to Connect, Facebook is a more formidable incumbent to networks such as Google+ that have entered Facebook's market.

While Facebook remains the number-one social network in terms of total monthly active users, with 1.11 billion as of first quarter 2013, Google+ has made some headway, jumping into the number-two spot above YouTube for the time first time in history. However, the words Google uses to describe the Google+ network could also be used to describe Facebook. They use words such as "social spine" and say that it "weaves" Google's products together, a la Connect. Just like Connect, Google+ is a single sign-on system that pulls together log-ins from Gmail, YouTube, and Blogger into one. And like Connect, Google+ can mine user data with the best of them. Keep in mind, however, that Facebook's active user base is currently 10 times that of Google+'s. That's like a sumo weighing 1,000 pounds going up against one that weighs 100 pounds. It's no contest.

But it's no contest because of the degree to which Facebook is now linked to so many other sumos via Connect. Taking down Facebook will be much, much harder thanks to its ties to its partners who rely on Connect to attract users and gather data about them. That's why Connect is Facebook's killer app.

APPLE'S KILLER APP

Another killer app example is Apple's iTunes service. What started out as a way to purchase and store electronic audio files has grown into a gateway that connects all Apple devices, linking iPhones to iPods to iPads to laptops and TVs. Introduce a non-Apple product into your gadget ecosystem and all that interconnectedness goes away, and no one wants that.

In iTunes' infancy, Apple computer desktops were the portal where music was downloaded and stored, via the iTunes software. Today, music, TV, and audio files are stored on the cloud via iTunes, downloadable to any Apple device. The interconnectedness that iTunes provides is a barrier to exit that few consumers ever want to face. Hence, this is the reason Apple product sales continue to grow year over year. Does any company have a chance of usurping iTunes in the near future? If you are a Mac user and have an iPhone, will you consider buying GoogleTV over the interconnected AppleTV? Not likely. You and your devices are too entrenched in the iTunes cloud.

Although Google's login and Google Play (formerly known as Android Market) are mimicking iTunes' business model, attempting to provide a service to link all Google properties and Android devices, Google is smarter than to go head-to-head against Apple. The market as a whole is squarely behind iTunes, and trying to push it out of the ring is guaranteed to be met with unwavering resistance. But providing that same connectedness to Android users makes a lot of sense. Don't take on one of the biggest sumos of all; simply train alongside them.

YOUR PATH TO A KILLER APP

As I said, not every company has a killer app. For a number of reasons, your business may not be in a position to develop and/or leverage a market-moving product. But it is very possible that you may actually have one and may not have recognized it yet. Or you may have a product that is light-years ahead of the competition and you use it to leapfrog them. Or you have the potential for a killer app but need the power of a sumo behind it to make it irresistible, to attract users in droves. Killer apps connect consumers with products or services and become so indispensable that demand quickly flips from push to pull, from trying to get customers to try it to hearing they can't live without it.

Killer apps integrate connectivity. They link consumers to your company and to others through a matrix, rather than a dotted or solid line, which is difficult to break through and eliminate. Once you're in it, it's hard to break free. In most cases, you have no interest in breaking free, because life is easier when you're using a killer app, such as iTunes or Connect. It's only when a more disruptive killer app comes along that you consider making a switch.

A KILLER APP IS A MIND-SET

So how do you start on the path toward developing a killer app? It begins internally, with a meeting of the minds within your company. Bringing together senior management for a working session designed to identify and examine the company's core competencies is step one. Where can you create leverage? What is your unique ability? Or what nugget of a killer app exists that you could build on and strengthen? That's what you need to be asking yourselves.

Those questions can then lead you to sumos to partner with. These would be companies that could catapult your business forward and make your core product line, for example, a killer app.

"SHOW ME THE CARFAX"

The Carfax Vehicle History Report has been used routinely by dealers for years to investigate how road worthy a particular car is based on available reported history before negotiating a trade or putting it on the car lot for sale. Instant access to timely information about a car is valuable to car shoppers and is a competitive advantage for dealers using Carfax. The report helps dealers communicate trust and confidence in purchasing a car, and that's the company's purpose. As a result, Carfax created a "Show me a free report" capability for its dealers so car shoppers can view the vehicle's history on any car listed for sale online or shown at a dealership. Carfax could have taken a product-focused path, as many companies do, and put their attention on improving the report itself. But instead, Carfax focused on enhancing the value of the report through continuous product improvements and also by enabling dealers to communicate trust when dealing with potential customers.

The challenge was that the functionality was not easily available anywhere. Dealers could cut and paste a URL into the free report, but that was laborious, inefficient, and plain old clunky. What Carfax needed to do was enable every website that advertises used vehicles for sale to embrace the instant report's functionality. The two giants on the top of the list were AutoTrader.com and Cars.com. The rest of that list consisted of hundreds of other sites, all of which required a partnership agreement, technical integration, and relationship management.

A daunting task. On the surface, many COOs may ask, "What's the ROI on this initiative compared with focusing on selling more reports through direct sales?" But digging deeper, there was a belief that it was good for the customer—both the consumer and the dealer. Fast-forward a couple of years and these Vehicle History Reports were available on virtually every website, including AutoTrader.com and Cars.com.

Today, Carfax is a household name, and its killer app is the Instant Vehicle History Report. Yes, a free report that all consumers can view so long as the report was paid for just once by a dealer. This killer app helped move the market toward Carfax. Coupled with its sales and marketing strategy, this killer app not only enabled more sales but also ensured that consumers now expect to see a Carfax report when they visit AutoTrader.com and Cars.com. Additionally, dealers now expect to see their cars listed on AutoTrader.com and Cars.com (and on their website, the OEM's site, and many other places inventory is showcased). This killer app is holding dealer retention and consumer demand in place. Carfax has turned this connection from "This is what is right for our customers" into a competitive advantage and, most importantly, a market-making solution.

Dealers may try to use a Carfax competitor that also has an instant report function, but those cars won't have the trusted and free Carfax report available for shoppers to view. If AutoTrader or Cars attempts to remove Carfax, they will create a market disconnect with dealers who rely on Carfax and with consumers who have grown to expect a free Carfax report. But as I mentioned in the last chapter, this symbiotic relationship cannot be sustained without a fair balance for all parties.

Once you create this type of dynamic with your killer app, it is important that you respect your partners and that they respect you. Don't try to exploit additional leverage at some point in the future. Not only is it not good business but also it provides an incentive to terminate the partnership, as no one likes being held hostage.

FROM PUSH TO PULL

Pushing a product, service, or technology out to a buying audience is typically how new concepts are marketed. Through education and promotion and brand management, potential customers are made aware of products and services that could benefit them. Those that see a need buy. That's a push marketing strategy. Yes, it works, but it's time consuming and expensive. A pull strategy is much more desirable.

Using a pull strategy, potential customers create demand for your latest product or service by expressing interest in buying. They then turn to typical outlets for your offering and ask how they can purchase it. Think of the customers standing in line at Apple stores waiting for the chance to own an iPhone 5 or parents hunting down the elusive Wii entertainment system the year that it debuted. The cost to market declines significantly when customers are ready and eager to buy.

In BD, transitioning from a push market strategy to a pull market strategy takes a partner (a sumo) to help spread the word and create demand. The sumo, with their presence and resources, can make inroads that smaller, entrepreneurial ventures rarely can. Without that sumo partner, you may be overlooked and never achieve enough customer demand to pull the product into other distribution outlets.

From a strategic perspective, integrating with another company starts to "pull" you forward. If many of your target customers rely on another company for systems, technology, fulfillment mechanisms, logistics, etc., and you partner with that company to solve a pain point, then you have not only differentiated yourself but also made your customer's choice to select you more compelling. This can quickly shift your whole marketing and sales strategy from push to pull, from trying to convince clients "You want us" to having them say "We want you."

12

FROM PLANNING
TO EXECUTION

You now have a big advantage. You understand that BD deals are strategic, not transactional. No longer will you send a sales account person to pitch a BD deal; you know sales and BD are both essential to your company but require different skill sets. Nor will you focus too quickly on direct revenue generation when partnering with a sumo that can transform your company. You realize it can take up to three years for serious revenue to materialize. And in your BD pitches, you don't rush to get a yes; instead, you focus on moving ahead simply by not getting a no. By successfully aligning yourself with a sumo, you can borrow credibility, create an entirely new revenue stream for both companies, and achieve exponential growth that can double or triple your company's valuation.

So where do you start? Start by thinking big picture. Really big. Imagine what your company would look like if you were a major player in your industry. Who would you be partnered with? What kinds of deals would you be working on? How would the industry, as a whole, be different from the way it is now? Who has the power?

In chapter 3, I suggested that you should think reactively to jump-start your brainstorming process. That is, consider what your worst nightmare would be with respect to your competition. What sumo could they partner with or what deal could they forge that would completely shut you out or be extremely damaging? What capability could they acquire that would be a near deathblow to your business? What are you most afraid of? Now flip this around and go after those deals. If such a partnership would be disastrous for you, it would likely be equally disastrous to your competition. That's a good start.

Thinking along those lines should help you create a preliminary list of potential sumos to approach, if you haven't approached them already. That's where you can begin to apply what you've learned to real-life business scenarios. I can almost guarantee you that there are one or two sumos you *should* be talking to.

So which sumo could provide access to a new market or to your current market but in a more efficient or effective way? If you run a start-up, which sumo could give you instant credibility to help you be taken seriously by other major players in your market? Pull your team together to brainstorm about whom you should be talking to.

Of course, identifying your top sumo targets is one thing, but being ready to partner with them is another. If the only people within your company to have agreed to pursue BD partnerships are those on your BD team, you have a problem. You can't start discussions with sumos unless your whole company is on board, from the top down, because landing that sumo could be your worst mistake if you don't already have buy-in from your senior executives; you'll need their support to be successful. Not only do you need a commitment of people—your BD team, which may be only you at the outset—but also you need a commitment of internal resources. That may be information technology (IT) support, or it may be marketing support, or it may even be financial if you end up having to make some guarantees down the line to assuage your sumo's nerves.

Once you have your company's support and have identified sumos that are appropriate partners for where your company is headed, it's time to start developing your pitch to them. Exactly what are you going to propose? What kind of product or service will you develop together? What customer segment can you help them serve? You need to have a presentation that outlines how you'll work together and—most important to them—what it will mean for their bottom line.

You need to approach any sumo with an idea of how you could work together, rather than make a vague suggestion that "maybe it would make sense to partner." "Why?" is likely to be their response if your pitch is so nebulous and weak. You won't get very far. You need to have a strong idea to propose from the outset.

While you aren't aiming to get approval for your proposal right off the bat, you also don't want to get shut down with a no. Paint a picture of what the two companies could do together, what it would mean for both in terms of potential revenue, and the impact on the industry. Be confident in your vision and you will inspire confidence in others.

When you finally do go for the yes, make sure it's with a term sheet. As we discussed earlier, hold off on getting the lawyers involved until that's done. Make sure your multiyear relationship is balanced and fair to both parties, and pick up the deal pace at this point. Otherwise, time starts to work against you.

ACTION ITEMS

So what do you do first, exactly? Here are your action items to get you started in exploring BD deals with your most desirable sumos:

1. Schedule a meeting with your senior management to confirm their support of strategic BD deals. Explain what, exactly, that could mean, including little or no direct revenue for at least a year. Have each of them answer the two questions on p 31.

2. Brainstorm what a worst-case scenario would look like with respect to your competitors. What could they do that would be extremely damaging to your business? Whom could they partner with? What capability could they build or procure?

3. Using that worst-case scenario as a springboard, next brainstorm with your team what your company could do to leapfrog your competition. Whom could you partner with? What products or services could you develop?

4. After prioritizing your best sumo targets, outline what your pitch would be. What kind of relationship do you want to develop? How would you work together to take advantage of each company's strengths and assets?

5. Armed with a proposal, start networking to find contacts within the sumo company to pitch. Start the conversation and build momentum and support internally. Once you get that first meeting, you're on your way.

BD isn't a new process, but I'm convinced that only a few companies are applying BD principles properly. That's why so many BD initiatives fail. However, if you follow this approach, you can be successful. It will take time—that I assure you—but it can be done.

CONCLUSION

For the past 20 years or so, a corporation's greatest fear was the 800-pound gorilla in their market. The gorilla, which typically held a majority market share, was perceived as unstoppable. Insurmountable. Which is why market leaders typically remained market leaders for years.

Those were the days of bloated corporations, fax machines, and three-martini lunches. Business deals were done on the golf course, and the odds of an entrepreneurial venture lasting more than five years were slim.

A lot has changed in the past 20 years.

For one, the pace of business has quickened to lightning speed. In the course of a three-martini lunch, which is now all but extinct, executives can be replaced and new technologies revolutionized, and stocks can rise to make shareholders millionaires. It's a different world. To get ahead and stay ahead in this kind of environment, companies can't operate the way they've always operated.

Fortunately, another shift that has occurred since the late 1990s is the rise of BD. Savvy companies, large and small, are now partnering to leverage each other's strengths. Start-ups are relying on heftier strategic teammates to leapfrog their competition. But those strategic teammates aren't gorillas. No, they are sumos. Gorillas went out of favor when it was realized they were large but not tactical enough. Enter the sumo.

Today, entrepreneurs that leverage the Sumo Advantage are thriving. They are researching, identifying, and cooperating with like-minded market leaders to enable their companies to best the competition. The Sumo Advantage is a critical tool that can provide massive growth, be a valuation multiplier, and position entrepreneurial ventures for hypergrowth and success.

But first you have to get a sumo to let you in their ring when they don't believe they need you. You can do it, of course, using the processes I've just outlined. And both companies will dominate in the business ring.

I'd love to hear about your wins. Please send me your success stories at **sumoadvantage@berniebrenner.com** and visit **www.Bernie Brenner.com** to get additional information, including assessment tools and worksheets, on growing your BD initiatives.

ABOUT THE AUTHOR

Bernie Brenner enjoys the development of new businesses and markets. He specializes in securing and expanding strategic partnerships and is a frequent speaker on business development (BD) to entrepreneurs and venture investors.

He is the co-founder and EVP of Business Development of TrueCar, Inc., a company focused on changing how cars are sold. Under Bernie's direction, TrueCar secured more than 100 BD deals, including partnerships with USAA, American Express, Geico, Nationwide Insurance, Consumer Reports, and AAA, generating over $100 million in annual revenue. Bernie is also a partner at the Capital Factory, an incubator/accelerator in Austin, Texas, where he is a mentor to many early stage entrepreneurs. Previously, Bernie ran business development at Carfax, Inc., where he secured partnerships with Toyota Motor Sales, AutoTrader.com, Cars.com and many other giants in the auto industry. He was the CEO of PromiseMark, Inc., an Internet security and privacy company, which he founded in 1997 by partnering with Symantec, maker of Norton Antivirus, and with Aon Warranty Group. He sold PromiseMark to a credit reporting agency in 2003. Bernie lives in Austin, Texas, with his wife and three children.